Book of Enoch: Angels, Watchers and Nephilim
Dr. A. Nyland

Book of Enoch: Angels, Watchers and Nephilim
Dr. A. Nyland
Copyright © 2010 by Dr A. Nyland
All Rights Reserved
ISBN 9781451561968

All translations are by Dr. A. Nyland unless otherwise noted.

*Under the auspices of the Morrigu.*

# Table of Contents.

# Chapter 1: Introduction

The *Book of Enoch* contains accounts of the Watchers, a class of angel, who came to earth, taught humans weapons, spell potions, root cuttings, astrology, and astronomy, and alchemies. The Watchers also slept with human women and produced the Nephilim. For this, they were punished by being bound and cast into the gloom of Tartarus. This is also mentioned in the New Testament.

The *Book of Enoch* is usually called 1 Enoch, to distinguish it from the later *The Secrets of Enoch*, also known as 2 Enoch. 1 Enoch is also called the *Ethiopic Enoch*, and 2 Enoch is also known as *Slavonic Enoch*, after the languages of the earliest versions extant of each respectively. No manuscript of the original language of either has as yet been discovered.

The authorship is contentious, but there is general agreement that several authors contributed to what we now call the *Book of Enoch*. Enoch was the son of Jared, great grandfather of Noah, and father of Methuselah, not to be confused with the Enoch who was the eldest son of Cain. (*1*)

The *Book of Enoch* was left out of the Canon, but a lengthy passage from the *Book of Enoch* is quoted by Jude. This cast doubts upon Jude's inclusion in the New Testament canon. Tertullian considered that the *Book of Enoch* should be included in the canon. The third century Bible translator Jerome stated, "Jude, James' brother, left a short letter which is considered among the seven broad letters, and because in it he quotes from the apocryphal book of Enoch it is rejected by many. Nonetheless by age and use it has gained authority and is considered among the Holy Scriptures." (*2*)

Many ancient sources referred to the *Book of Enoch*, but it was not until 1773 that James Bruce discovered three copies in Ethiopia.

## Chapter 2: The Book of Enoch
## The Book of the Watchers

**1:1-9.**

The word of the blessing of Enoch, how he blessed the chosen ones and the just, who were to live in the time of trouble, rejecting all the wicked who would be removed.

Enoch was a just person, whose eyes were opened by God, and saw a sacred vision in the heavens and told about it. The angels showed me this. I heard everything from them, and understood what I saw. It will not take place in this generation, but in a generation which will come at a future point.

### *Angels.*

*Angels were actually "messengers." "Angel" is transliteration of the Greek word, and not a translation. To "transliterate" (noun, "transliteration") means to put the Greek letters into English letters. "Angels" is the transliteration but the meaning is "messengers." The Hebrew word for "angel" actually means one dispatched as a deputy. The word occurs for an ordinary messenger as well as a supernatural messenger. (3)*

*I spoke, and conversed with him about the chosen ones. The sacred mighty one will leave his dwelling. The eternal God will tread on the earth, on Mount Sinai. He will appear with his hosts, and appear with his powerful strength from heaven. Everyone will be afraid, and the Watchers (4) will be terrified. Great fear and trembling will grip them, as far as to the ends of the earth. The high mountains will be shaken, and the high hills brought low, melting like wax in the flame. The earth will be ripped open, and everything in it will perish, and there will be judgment on all. But he will give peace to the just. He will safeguard the chosen and show them compassion. Then they will all belong to God and they will be prosperous and blessed. His light will appear to them. The Lord comes with tens of thousands of his devoted people, to carry out judgments on everyone, to cross-examine every soul among them who has committed sacrilege, about their sacrilegious acts, and about all the harsh things that sacrilegious wrongdoers have said about him.*

*This was quoted by Jude in the New Testament, verses 14-15: " (14) Now Enoch, the seventh from Adam, prophesied to these people too. He said, 'The Lord comes with tens of thousands of his devoted people, (15) to carry out judgments on everyone, to cross-examine every soul among them who has committed sacrilege, about their sacrilegious acts, and about all the harsh things that sacrilegious wrongdoers have said about him.' (16) These people are complaining grumblers going the way of their own wants and wishes. They boast excessively about themselves, and flatter other people for their own benefit."*

## 2:1-3

All who are in the heavens know what happens there. They know that the heavenly luminaries do not change their paths, that each rises and sets regularly at the proper time, without wandering off from their appointed order. Observe the earth, and take notice of what happens there, from the beginning to the end, how nothing changes, but God's work is apparent. Observe the summer and winter, how the whole earth is full of water, and that the cloud, the dew, and the rain lie on it.

## 3:1.

Observe how every tree appears to wither and shed its leaves, except for fourteen trees, which are not deciduous but retain their old leaves for two or three winters until the new leaves appear.

## 4:1.

And again, observe the days of summer, how the sun is on it at the very beginning, while you look for a covered and shady spot due to the burning sun. The earth burns with scorching heat, and because of that heat you cannot walk on the ground or the rocks.

**5:6-9.**

Observe how the trees cover themselves with green leaves and produce fruit. Observe that he who lives for ever has made all these things, and that his works continue from year to year, and that all the tasks they do for him do not change, but things are brought to pass as God has appointed them to do so.

Observe how the seas and the rivers together do what they are meant to do. But you have not been unwavering, nor have you carried out the Lord's instructions, but you have misbehaved and spoken nasty, spiteful words with your polluted mouths against his magnificence You hard hearted, no peace will come to you! Therefore you will curse your days, and your lives will come to an end, you will be the object of increasing and perpetual cursing, and you will not find compassion.

In those times, all the just will consider your names to be an abhorrent curse, and all who curse, will curse by you. All the wrongdoers and the unjust will invoke evil by you, and for you, the godless, there will be a curse. Then they will celebrate, and there will be forgiveness for wrongdoings, and compassion, peace and tolerance. There will be rescue for them, a good light. But on you all there will be a curse. But for the chosen ones there will be light, favor, and peace, and they will inherit the earth.

Wisdom will be given to the chosen ones. They will live and not do wrong whether through godlessness or pride, but the wise ones will be humble. They will not do wrong again for the rest of their lives. They will not die as result of anger or torment, but will live out the full term of their lives. They will grow old in peace, while their lives will increase with happiness, and with peace, for all the days of their lives.

**6:1-8.**

It happened after the humans (5) had multiplied, that in those times daughters were born to them, and they were attractive and beautiful.

## So called "Sons of God," "Daughters of men."

The phrase often mistranslated "sons of men," "children of men," actually meant "people," "humans." The word children/sons with a noun refers to a member of a class of people, and should not be translated as "son/child of." The phrase "sons of (place name)" /"children of (place name)" again refers to inhabitants of that place. The Benai Israel, translated in the King James Version as "children/sons of Israel" actually means "members of the class of people called Israel" and should be translated as "Israelites." The expression is also Greek, and found as early as Homer. The same is the case in the New Testament, where the Greek word huios is placed with the word "Israel," referring to "members of the class of people called Israel" and should be translated as "Israelites." Properly, it is not to be translated "children of Israel" or "sons of Israel." Likewise, Autenrieth's Homeric Dictionary notes that huios with the word Achaeon means "Achaeans" and this is typical Greek usage.

The word huios is often used with a noun to express a similarity with the noun. For example, an ancient Greek would put the word huios (son, child) with a word meaning "perfume" to mean "the perfumed one" or to refer to a person who smells nice. In word-for-word Greek, the same expression would appear as "child/son of Perfume," but such a (mis)translation is not the correct meaning. Sometimes Greek simply used the genitive case instead of inserting the word huios. For example, in Aristophanes' (the famous comic playwright of the 5th century B.C.) play Acharnians, 1150, Antimachon ton Psakados appears to be word-for-word "Antimachos child/son of showers" but proper translation method demands we translate as "Antimachos the spitter" or similar. The scholia states that he was so-named because he spat when speaking and "showered spray on those who were talking to him."

The standard ancient Greek language lexicon (dictionary) Liddell-Scott(-Jones) lists the meanings for huios as 1. son, 2. with a place name simply to mean inhabitants of the place name, 3. children, 4. used with numbers of years to indicate age, as well as several other meanings.

Thus "sons of God" is a mistranslation for "associates of God", and "daughters of men" is a mistranslation for "human women."

When the angels, (6) the inhabitants of heaven, saw them, they lusted after them and said to each other, "Come on, let's choose consorts for ourselves from the humans, and let's produce children!"

### Inhabitants of heaven/Associates of God

This expression refers to the inhabitants of heaven. Both the ancient Rabbis and the Church fathers did not acknowledge bene ha 'elohim as "associates of God," (properly, "associates of Elohim"). The Rabbis saw them as righteous men and the Church Fathers saw them as Seth's descendants.

**Job 2:1**

*Again there was a day when the associates of God came to present themselves before Yahweh, and Satan also came with them to present himself before Yahweh.*

**Job 38:7**

*When the morning stars sang together, and all the associates of God shouted for joy?*

**Psalm 29:1**

*A psalm of David.*

*Assign to Yahweh, you mighty ones (bene 'elim), assign to him splendor and strength!*

**Psalm 89:7**

*El is respected in the great assembly of the sacred ones,*

*he is more awe-inspiring than all who surround him.*

Then their leader Semjaza (7) said to them, "I'm concerned as I fear that perhaps you won't agree to carry out this venture, and that I alone will have to pay the penalty for such a serious crime."

But they answered, "Let's all swear an oath, and bind ourselves by mutual curses, that we will not change our minds but carry through this venture."

So they swore all together and bound themselves by mutual curses. They were two hundred in number, they descended in the time of Jared, (8) on the top of Mount Hermon. They called it Mount Hermon because they had sworn an oath on it and bound themselves by mutual curses. (9)

11

## Leader of the Watchers

### Account in 2 Enoch

*"These are the Grigori, who with their chief Satanail rejected the Lord of light, and after them are those who are held in the great darkness on the second heaven, and three of them went down on earth to the place Hermon, and broke their vows on the shoulder of the Mount Hermon and saw the human women, and slept with them, and contaminated the earth with their deeds. In their times they caused lawless mixing, and Nephilim were born, amazing big people, and great hostility. So God judged them strongly, and they weep for their associates. They will be punished on the Lord's great day." (2 Enoch 18:3-4.)*

### Account in Psalms.

### Psalm 82

*A psalm of Asaph.*

*1 Elohim presides over the assembly of El, (10)*

*he gives judgment in the midst of the elohim: (11)*

*2 "How long will you defend the unjust and show favoritism to the wicked? Selah*

*3 Defend the cause of the poor and the fatherless,*

*defend the rights of the oppressed and suffering.*

*4 Rescue the poor and needy, rescue them from the power of the wicked.*

*5 They know nothing, they understand nothing,*

*they walk around in the dark, all the foundations of the earth are shaken.*

*6 I said, 'You are elohim,*

*all of you are associates of Elyon.'*

*7 Yet you will die like mortals,*

*you will fall like the other rulers."*

*8 Rise up, Elohim, and judge the earth,*

*for you own all the nations.*

### Account in Isaiah 14:12-21

"How you are fallen from heaven, Lucifer, (12) associate of dawn! How you are cut down to the ground, you who weakened the nations!"

"For you said to yourself, 'I will ascend to heaven and set my throne above El's stars. I will preside on the appointed mountain in the sides of the north. I will climb to above the height of the clouds, I will be like Elyon.'

"But instead, you will be brought down to Sheol, to the sides of the pit. Everyone there will stare at you and ask, 'Is this the one who shook the earth and the kingdoms of the world, that made the world a wilderness and demolished its cities and did not free the prisoners from Sheol?'

"The kings of the nations lie in splendid tombs, but you will be thrown out of your grave like a ritually abominable branch. You will be dumped like the remainder of those slain by the sword with those killed in battle like a corpse trampled underfoot, you will go down to the dungeon. You will not be given a proper burial, because you have destroyed your land and killed your people. The offspring of evildoers will never be proclaimed. Kill the children of this wrongdoer so they do not rise and conquer the land or rebuild the cities of the world."

### Account in Ezekiel 28:11-19

"The word of Yahweh came to me, 'Human, weep for the king of Tyre and say to him, "Adonai Yahweh says, 'You were full of wisdom and beauty. You were in Eden, Elohim's garden. Your clothing had every precious stone: sardius, chrysolite, diamond, beryl, onyx, jasper, sapphire, and emerald, carbuncle, gold, and the making of the settings was crafted for you on the day you were created.

'You are the anointed cherub that defends. You had access to Elohim's sacred mountain and walked among the fiery stones. You were complete in everything you did from the day you were created until the day injustice was found in you.

'Your great wealth filled you with violence, and you sinned. So I banished you from Elohim's mountain. Mighty guardian, I expelled you from your place among the fiery stones. Your heart was filled with pride because of your beauty. You corrupted your wisdom

13

*because of your splendor. So I threw you to the earth and exposed you to the gaze of kings.*

*'You defiled your sanctuaries with your many wrongdoings and your dishonest trade. So I brought fire from within you, and it consumed you. I will burn you to ashes on the ground in the sight of all who are watching. All who knew you are appalled at your destruction. You have come to a terrible end, and you are no more."*

### Account in Luke 10:17-20

*The seventy came back and were very happy. They said, "Lord, even the demons yield to us in your name!"*

*"Yes, I know," Jesus replied. "I was watching Adversary fall like a flash of lightning from the sky. I have given you the authority to trample on snakes and scorpions, and authority over all the enemy's power, and nothing will harm you. But all that aside, don't be happy just because the spirits yield to you, but instead be happy that your names have been written down in the heavenly places."*

### Account in Revelation

**Ch.12:1-2** *And a mighty sign appeared in heaven. It was a woman clothed with the sun, with the moon under her feet and a crown of twelve stars on her head.* **2** *She was pregnant, and cried out in torture as she was in labor and about to give birth.*

**3-6** *And I saw another sign in heaven. It was a huge red dragon with seven heads, ten horns, and seven diadems on the heads!* **4** *Its tail dragged a third of the stars out of the sky and hurled them to the earth. The dragon stood in front of the woman who was about to give birth, so that he could eat her child the moment it was born.* **5** *She gave birth to a son, who is destined to rule all the nations with an iron rod. Her child was snatched away and carried up to God and to his throne.* **6** *The woman escaped into the desert to a place that God had prepared for her, so that she would be taken care of for 1,260 days.*

**7-9** *War broke out in heaven. Michael and his Messengers waged war against the dragon, and the dragon and his messengers fought back.* **8** *But the dragon wasn't strong enough, and thus they no longer had a place in heaven.* **9** *The mighty dragon was thrown down - that ancient snake called "Slanderer-Liar", and also called*

*"Adversary," who leads the whole earth astray. He and his Messengers were hurled to the earth.*

***10-12*** *Then I heard a loud voice in heaven saying: "Just now have come salvation and power and the kingdom realm of our God, and the authority of his Anointed One. Because the accuser of our fellow believers, who accuses them in front of our God day and night has been hurled down.* ***11*** *And they conquered him by the Blood of the Lamb and by the Message of their testimony. They were willing to give up their lives.* ***12*** *For this reason rejoice, you heavenly places and those who encamp in them. But alas for the earth and the sea, because Slanderer-Liar has gone down to you! He is in a major rage, because he knows the time is short!"*

***13-18*** *And when the dragon realized that it had been hurled to the earth, it chased the woman who had given birth to the male child.*

***14*** *The woman was given the two wings of a huge eagle, so that she could fly to the place prepared for her in the desert. In that place she would be taken care of for a time, times, and half a time.* ***15*** *And the snake spat out water like a river from its mouth, in order to overtake the woman and sweep her away in the current.* ***16*** *The earth helped the woman by swallowing the river that the dragon had spat out of its mouth.* ***17*** *The dragon was furious with the woman and went off to make war against the rest of her offspring - those who obey God's commandments and hold onto to Jesus' testimony.* ***18*** *And the dragon stood on the seashore.*

These are the names of their leaders: Semjaza, who was their leader, Arakiba, Rameel, Kokaqbiel, Ramuel, Tamiel, Ramiel, Danel, Ezeqeel, Baraqijal, Asael, Armaros, Batarerl, Ananel, Zaqiel, Samsapeel, Satarei, Turel, Jomjael, Sariel. (*13*) These were the leaders of the groups of ten.

### Account in the Book of Jubilees: God sent the Watchers to earth

*"And in the second week of the tenth jubilee Mahalalel took Dinah as a wife. She was the daughter of Barakiel, the daughter of his father's brother, and she bore him a son in the third week of the sixth year. He named him Jared, and in his days the Lord's angels named the Watchers came down to the earth, in order to instruct the*

15

*humans, and so that they could carry out judgment and justice on the earth." (Jubilees 4:15)*

*God was exceedingly angry against the angels he had sent upon the earth. (Jubilees 5:6)*

## 7:1-6.

They and the rest took consorts. Each one chose their own. They had sex with them and defiled themselves with them. They taught them charms and sorceries, the cutting of roots, and the uses of plants.

The women got pregnant and gave birth to Nephilim (<u>14</u>) whose height was three hundred cubits. They consumed everything humans produced. When humans could no longer sustain them, they turned against them, in order to consume them. They began to do wrong against birds, beasts, reptiles, and fish, and to eat each other's flesh, (<u>15</u>) and to drink their blood. Then the earth laid accusation against the lawless ones.

### *Parallel accounts in the Hebrew Bible / Old Testament*
### *Parallel account in Genesis 6:1-4*

*Genesis 6:1-4: "When humankind began to increase on the face of the earth, and daughters were born to them, those associated with God (<u>16</u>) saw that the human women were beautiful and so they took wives for themselves from any they chose. ... The Nephilim were on the earth in those times, and also afterwards, when those associated with God were having sex with the human women, who gave birth to their children. They were the Gibborim of ancient times, the famous ones."*

*The Septuagint, Philo of Alexandria, Josephus, Justin Martyr, Irenaeus, Athenagoras, Clement of Alexandria, Tertullian, Lactantius, Eusebius, Ambrose of Milan, Jerome, Sulpicius Severus, and Augustine of Hippo all identified the "Sons of God" (correctly, "the associates of God") of Genesis 6:1-4 with the angels who came to earth and had sex with human women.*

### *Nephilim in Numbers 13:33*

The word "Nephilim" occurs only twice in the Old Testament /Hebrew Bible, in Genesis 6:4 (see above) and Numbers 13:33. Here is the mention in Numbers 13:33: "And there we saw the Nephilim (the Anakims, who come from the Nephilim), and we seemed to ourselves to be like grasshoppers, and we seemed the same to them."

For some reason, the word "Nephilim" is translated by the English word "giants" in several Bible versions. The word "Rephaim" is also translated by the English word "giants" in several Bible versions.

### Deuteronomy 2:11

Like the Anakims, they too were considered Rephaim, but the Moabites called them Emims.

### Deuteronomy 2:20

That area, too, was once considered to be the land of the Rephaim, and the Ammonites referred to them as Zamzummims.

### 2 Samuel 21:20

In still another battle, which took place at Gath, there was a man of stature with six fingers on each hand and six toes on each foot, twenty-four in all. He also was descended from the Rephaim.

### Deuteronomy 3:11

King Og of Bashan was the last of the Rephaim. His iron bed was more than 9 cubits (13 feet = 4.1 meters) long and 4 cubits (6 feet = 1.8 meters) wide. It remains today in the Ammonite city of Rabbah.

Deuteronomy 3:13

I gave the rest of Gilead and also all of Bashan, the kingdom of Og, to the half tribe of Manasseh. The whole region of Argob in Bashan used to be known as a land of the Rephaim.

Note: Goliath is often said to be one of the Nephilim, but there is no evidence for this. As we have seen, the two passages in Old Testament / Hebrew Bible which mention Nephilim have nothing to do with Goliath.

### 1 Samuel 17:4.

"And a champion went out from the camp of the Philistines. He name was Goliath, and he was from Gath, and his height was six cubits and a span."

*Note: The Septuagint, the Dead Sea Scrolls, and Josephus have his height as 4 cubits and a span, which is 6 ¾ feet tall (2 meters). Six cubits and span is 9 feet tall. However, Goliath was not called a Nephilim.*

## 8:1-4.

Azazel taught humans to make swords, knives, shields, breastplates, and showed them metals of the earth and the art of alchemy, and bracelets and ornaments, the use of antimony and paint, the beautifying of the eyelids, the use of all types of precious stones, and all sorts of dyes. Then wickedness and immorality increased, and they disobeyed, and everything they did was corrupt.

Semjaza taught spell potions, and root cuttings,

 Armaros taught the resolving of spell potions,

Baraqijal taught astrology,

Kokabel taught the constellations,

Ezeqeel taught the knowledge of the clouds,

Araqiel the signs of the earth,

Shamseil the signs of the sun,

and Sareil the course of the moon.

And as humans perished, they cried out, and their voice reached heaven.

### *Azazel*

*Azazel is mistranslated "scapegoat" by several Bible versions, a mistranslation started by Tyndale's 16th century English translation and followed by such versions as the King James Version, and the New International Version. It is translated correctly as "Azazel" in the Revised Standard Version and the English Standard Version. Tyndale misread the Hebrew word to mean "escaped goat" and coined the word "scapegoat."*

*The name Azazel occurs 3 times in the Old Testament /Hebrew Bible, in Leviticus 16: 8, 10, 26. The context is that on Yom Kippur, the Day of Atonement, the high priest performed the set sacrifices for himself and his family then presented the victims for the sins of*

18

the people. These were a ram for the burnt offering, and two young goats for the sin-offering. The high priest brought the goats before Yahweh at the door of the tabernacle, and cast lots for them, one lot "for Yahweh" and the other lot "for Azazel." The goat that fell by lot to Yahweh was killed as a sin-offering for the people. The high priest laid his hands on the head of the goat that fell by lot to Azazel and confessed the sins of the people over it. The goat was then handed over to a man who led it to an isolated region and let it go in the wilderness.

**Leviticus 16:6:** "Aaron will offer the bull as a sin offering for himself and shall make atonement for himself and for his family.

7 Then he will take the two goats and set them before the Lord at the entrance of the tent of meeting. 8 And Aaron will cast lots over the two goats, one lot for the Lord and the other lot for Azazel. 9 And Aaron will present the goat on which the lot fell for the Lord and use it as a sin offering, 10 but the goat on which the lot fell for Azazel will be presented alive before the Lord to make atonement over it, and it will be sent away into the wilderness to Azazel. ......

26 And he who lets the goat go to Azazel will wash his clothes and bathe his body in water, and then afterwards he may come back into the camp."


The 13th century Nahmanides' (Rabbi Moses ben Nachman's) commentary on Leviticus 26:8 states that Azazel belongs to the class of se'irim, hairy goat like demons. This follows Rabbi Abraham ibn Ezra's commentary although Ibn Ezra did not state this explicitly. Isaiah 34:15 states, "The wild animals of the desert will meet with the howlers, and the hairy goat demon (se'irim) will cry to its fellow. Lilith will settle there and find for herself a resting place." Isaiah 13:21 states, "But the desert dwellers will recline there, and their dwellings will be full of howling creatures, and female unclean birds (17) will live there, and hairy goat demons (se'irim) will dance there."

2 Chronicles 11:15 states, "And he appointed his own priests for the high places, and for the hairy goat demons (se'irim), and for the calf idols which he had made."

*The Septuagint (ancient Greek translation of the Hebrew scriptures), translates se'irim by an ancient Greek word meaning "profane" or "useless."*

*In the first to second century Jewish text (18) the Apocalypse of Abraham, Azazel is portrayed as an unclean bird which came down upon the sacrifice prepared by Abraham. (19) It describes Azazel as an evil spirit, a liar, and as an entity that brings troubles to humans who live wickedly. (20) The Apocalypse of Abraham states that the wicked will decay in the belly of the cunning worm Azazel, and be burned by the fire of Azazel's tongue." (21) Azazel's appearance is described as a dragon with hands and feet like a human's, and having six wings on the right and six wings on the left of his back." (22) God is said to share the earth with Azazel. (23)*

*Islam tradition holds Azazel as one of the Jinn. Jinn (or Djinn) are Arabian spiritual beings who are shape shifters, evil spirits, and treacherous spirits who can create illusions. They are creatures of flame and were created from smokeless fire and the searing wind. There are many different kinds of Jinn. Jinn are considered to be the cause of shooting stars, whirlwinds, and sandstorms. They prefer to live in desolate places.*

*In Islamic tradition, Azazel is identified with Iblis (Eblis).(24) The Qur'an states that when the angels were told to submit to Adam they did, but Iblis refused and was arrogant. (25) It also states that Iblis said Allah created him out of fire while humans were created out of clay, and that Allah banished him. (26)*

*This is an excerpt from the Islamic Twenty-first Discourse On Addressing Iblis the Accursed: "The Shaikh (may Allah be well pleased with him, and may He grant him contentment) said: I saw Iblis in a dream, where I was in the midst of a big crowd. I was on the point of killing him, when he said to me (may Allah curse him): 'Why are you going to kill me? What is my offense? If evil is entailed by destiny, I am powerless to change it and transform it into good, and if good is so entailed I cannot change it and transform it into evil. So what do I control?'*

*"Hermaphroditic in appearance, he was soft-spoken, with distorted features, wisps of hair on his chin, misshapen and deformed. When he smiled at me, the smile was bashful and apprehensive.*

*"This happened on the night of Sunday, 12th of Dhu'l-Hijja in the
year 516 [of the Hijra]. "Allah is the Guide to all that is good!"* (27)

## 9:1-11.

Then Michael, Uriel, Raphael, and Gabriel looked down from
heaven and saw much bloodshed on earth, and all the lawlessness
that was happening on the earth. They said one to another, "It's the
voice of their cries! The earth deprived of her children has cried as
far as the portal of heaven. And now people's souls complain to you,
you sacred ones of heaven! They say, "Bring our case to the Most
High!" Then they said to their Lord, "You are Lord of lords, God of
gods, King of kings. Your splendid throne lasts for ever and ever,
and is your name is sacred, magnificent, and blessed for ever and
ever. You have made everything and you have power over
everything, everything is open and clear before you. You see
everything, and nothing can be hidden from you.

### Gabriel in the New Testament

### *Luke 1*

*7 In the time of Herod, the king of Judea, there was a certain priest
named Zacharias. He was a member of the priestly order of Abijah.
His wife was one of the descendants of Aaron, and her name was
Elizabeth. 6 They were both right before God, and they acted
blamelessly as to all the commandments and regulations of the Lord.
7 But they didn't have any children, as Elizabeth was barren and
they were both getting on in years.*

*8-11 Now it turned out that while Zacharias was serving God with
his priestly duties when his priestly division was on duty, he was
chosen by lot – 9 this was in line with the priestly custom - to burn
incense when he went into the temple of the Lord. 10 At the time of
the incense offering, the whole crowd of people was praying outside.
11 A Messenger of the Lord appeared in front of him, standing on the
right side of the incense altar.* (28)

*12-17 When Zacharias saw him, he got all mixed up and he became
quite scared. 13 But the Messenger reassured him, "Zacharias,
don't be afraid! Your earnest request has been heard. Your wife
Elizabeth will bear you a son, and you must give him the name*

'John'. 14 He will be a joy and a delight to you, and lots of people will shout joyfully because of him. 15 He will be important in the Lord's sight! He'll never take wine or sweet fermented liquor and he will be filled with the Holy Spirit even from birth. 16 He will bring back many Israelites to the Lord their God. 17 He will go on ahead of the Lord to prepare people for the Lord. He will be equipped with the same spirit and power that Elijah had, to correct the attitudes of parents to their children. He will correct disobedient people so that they will have the common sense of the people who are right with God, and make ready for the Lord people who are well prepared for him."

18-20 "What's going to make me believe that this is the case! Zacharias asked the Messenger. "Me - I'm an old man, that's for sure, and my wife's well and truly getting on years!"

19 The Messenger answered, "I am Gabriel, who stands in the presence of God, and who was sent to announce this Good News to you! 20 Well then! You will be silent! As you didn't believe my words, which will in fact turn out just as I said, you won't be able to speak a word until the very day it actually happens!"

21-23 The people waited for Zacharias. They were surprised that he was spending such a long time in the temple. 22 When he came out, he couldn't speak to them. They realized that he had seen a vision, because he kept on making signs and stayed firmly speechless the whole time. 23 And it turned out that as soon as his time of priestly ministry was completed, he went back home.

24-25 After these events his wife Elizabeth became pregnant and lived in seclusion for five months. 25 "The Lord has done this for me!" she exclaimed. "He was watching over me to take away my inability to have children which the people considered to be a disgrace."

26-29 When Elizabeth was six months pregnant, God sent the Messenger Gabriel to Nazareth, a city in Galilee, 27 to an unmarried girl who was engaged to a man named Joseph, a descendant of David. The unmarried girl's name was Mary. 28 The Messenger greeted her, "Hello there, you highly favored person! The Lord is with you!" 29 But she was deeply disturbed and wondered what sort of greeting this was!

*30-38 The Messenger continued, "Don't be afraid, Mary! You've found favor with God! 31 You will become pregnant and give birth to a son, and you are to name him Jesus. 32 He will be very important, and will be called the Son of the Most High, and the Lord God will give him the throne of his ancestor David. 33 He will reign over the house of Jacob forever, and his Realm will never end."*

*34 "How can this be?" Mary asked the Messenger. "I'm a virgin: I haven't been with a man!"*

*35 The Messenger answered, "The Holy Spirit will come upon you and the power of the Most High will spread his shadow over you. The one to be born will be sacred and will be called the Son of God. 36 Your relative Elizabeth has also become pregnant with a son in her old age. They said she was unable to have children but now she is six months pregnant! 37 Every spoken word from God has power!"*

*38 "Fantastic!" Mary exclaimed. "I am the Lord's slave servant! May everything you've said come true!" And then the Messenger left her.*

## Gabriel in the Old Testament / Hebrew Bible

### Daniel 8:15-27

*Then it came about that when I, Daniel, had seen the vision and was looking for its meaning, that suddenly someone who looked like a human stood in front of me. I heard a human voice calling out from the Ulai river banks, "Gabriel, tell this man the meaning of the vision.*

*So he approached the place where I was standing and then I became terrified and I fell on my face. He said to me, "Human, understand that the events you have seen in your vision relate to the future."*

*Now, as he was speaking with me, I was in a deep sleep with my face to the ground, but he touched me, and stood me upright. He said, "I'm here to reveal to you what will happen later in angry times. What you have seen pertains to the very end of time. The two-horned ram you saw represents the kings of Media and Persia. The hairy goat demon you saw is the king of Ionia, and the large horn between its eyes is the first king. As for the horn that was broken, and the four others that took its place, four kingdoms will rise from that nation, but not by his power. And at the end time of their kingdom, when the wrongdoers have reached their limit, a king of bold appearance, one who understands enigmas, will arise. He will be very powerful but not by his own power. He will cause a huge amount of destruction and everything he does will succeed. He will destroy powerful leaders and devastate the sacred people. He will cunningly make deceitfulness prosper by his power, and he will praise himself. He will carelessly destroy many. He will rise up against the Leader of leaders, but in the end his power will be broken. The vision of the evening and morning that has been told to you is true, but hide the vision, as it's about the distant future."*

*And I, Daniel, was weak for several days. Afterwards I got up and attended to the king's business, but I was appalled by the vision and no one understood it.*

### Daniel 9:21-27

*While I was praying, the one Gabriel, whom I had seen in the vision at the beginning, ran swiftly, and approached me about the time of the evening offering.*

*He explained to me, "Daniel, I've come here to give you insight and understanding. At the beginning of your prayers the word went out, and I've come to report it to you, for you are loved. So discern the utterance and understand the vision. Seventy weeks are marked out for your people and your sacred city, to stop rebellion, to put wrongdoing to an end, to make atonement for crime, to bring in continual justice, and to hide the vision and prophecy, and to anoint the most sacred.*

*"So perceive and understand that from the going out of the word to restore and build Jerusalem to the coming of the anointed one, a prince, there will be seven weeks. Then for sixty-two weeks it will be built again with streets and moat, but in a time of distress. After the sixty-two weeks, the anointed one will be cut off and will have nothing. The people of the leader who is to come will destroy the city and the sanctuary. Its end will come with a flood, and devastations are decreed up to the end of the war. And he will cut a covenant with many for one week, and for half the week he will make the sacrifice and offering cease. He will devastate the edges of the detestable, until that which is decided is poured out on the devastator."*

## Michael in the New Testament

### Jude 9

*But Michael the Chief Messenger, when he was deciding the dispute, discoursing with Slanderer-Liar about Moses' body, did not dare to impose an abusive sentence on him, but said, "May the Lord impose the penalty on you!" (29)*

### Revelation 12

*7-9 War broke out in heaven. Michael and his Messengers waged war against the dragon, and the dragon and his Messengers fought back. 8 But the dragon wasn't strong enough, and thus they no longer had a place in heaven. 9 The mighty dragon was thrown down - that ancient snake called "Slanderer-Liar", and also called "Adversary," who leads the whole earth astray. He and his Messengers were hurled to the earth.*

## Michael in the Old Testament / Hebrew Bible

### Daniel 10:2-21

*In those days I, Daniel, was mourning for three weeks. I did not eat any tasty food, no meat or wine touched my lips, and I did not use any lotions at all until the three weeks were over. On the twenty-fourth day of the first month, as I was standing on the bank of the great river, the Tigris, I looked up and there in front of me was a man dressed in linen, and wearing a belt of fine gold from Uphaz around his waist.*

*His body was like a precious yellow gemstone, his face shone like lightning, his eyes were like fiery torches, his arms and legs gleamed like burnished bronze, and his voice sounded like a crowd of people speaking.*

*I, Daniel, was the only one who saw the vision. The people with me did not see it, but such fear came on them that they fled and hid themselves. So I was left alone and saw this great vision. No strength was left in me. My vigor was completely destroyed and I had no strength at all. Then I heard the sound of his words, and when I heard the sound of his words, I was on my face in a deep sleep with my face to the ground. A hand touched me which shook me to my knees and on the palms of my hands!*

He said to me, "Daniel, you greatly loved person, discern the words I'm about to tell you, and stand up! I have now been sent to you."

When he said this to me, I stood up shuddering. Then he said to me, "Don't be afraid, Daniel. Since the first day you began to pray for understanding and to be occupied with Elohim's presence, your words were heard, and I've come because of your words. But the spirit leader of the kingdom of Persia withstood me for twenty-one days, but Michael, one of the foremost spirit leaders, came to help me, as I was left there with the spirit kings of Persia. Now I've come to explain to you what will happen to your people in the future, for the vision concerns a time yet to come. Now I've come so you will discern what will happen to your people in the future, as the vision is about the future."

When he said this to me, I bowed with my face toward the ground and I was unable to speak. Then the one who looked like a human (30) touched my lips, and I opened my mouth and spoke. I said to the one standing in front of me, "I'm utterly distressed by the vision, and my strength has left me! How can someone like me, your master's servant, talk to you, my master? I have no strength left, and I can hardly breathe."

Then the one who looked like a human touched me again and gave me strength. He said, "Don't be afraid, you loved person. Be at peace, be strong, be strong!"

As he spoke these words, I suddenly grew stronger and said to him, "Now please speak, my master, you've strengthened me."

He replied, "Do you know why I've come? Soon I have to return to fight against the spirit prince of the kingdom of Persia, and then when I have left, the spirit leader of the kingdom of Ionia will come! But I will tell you what is written in the truthful writings, and there is no one who supports me against these except Michael, your spirit leader."

### Daniel 12:1

"At that time Michael, the great spirit leader who takes a stand for your people, will take a stand. There will be a time of trouble such as has not happened from the beginning of nations until then. But at that time your people - those whose names are found written in the book - will escape."

### Raphael and Uriel

*Raphael and Uriel are not mentioned in the Old Testament / Hebrew Bible or the New Testament. Raphael features strongly in the Book of Tobit, a book of scripture that is part of the Catholic and Orthodox Biblical canon, and found in the Septuagint, the ancient Greek Old Testament/Hebrew Bible text from the 3rd to 2nd centuries BC, which was translated from the Hebrew texts of the times. The Septuagint is quoted in the New Testament. It was widely used by the Hellenistic Jews of the era.*

*Hebrew and Aramaic fragments of the Book of Tobit were discovered in Cave IV at Qumran in 1952. The Book of Tobit was put forward by the Council of Carthage of 397 and confirmed for Roman Catholics in 1546 by the Council of Trent. Tobit is considered apocryphal by Protestants, and was not included as canon by ancient Judaism.*

*In the Book of Tobit, Raphael tells Tobit that God sent him to cure his blindness and to help his daughter-in-law Sara as the evil spirit Asmodeus had killed her 7 husbands. (31) The Book of Tobit 3:17 states, "Raphael was sent to heal them both, that is, to scale away the whiteness of Tobit's eyes, and to give Sara the daughter of Raguel as a wife to Tobias, Tobit's son, and to bind the evil spirit Asmodeus."*

*The Book of Tobit 12:15 states, "I am Raphael, one of the seven sacred angels who present the prayers of the people devoted to God, and I go in and out in the presence of the splendor of the Sacred One."*

*Raphael is not mentioned in the Qur'an.*

*Raphael, Gabriel, Uriel and Michael are all mentioned in The Testament of Solomon. The Testament of Solomon is an Old Testament pseudepigraphical work, said to be, as the name suggests, written by King Solomon. It describes how Solomon was able to build the Temple by commanding demons, thanks to a ring given to him by the archangel Michael.*

*When a demon named Ornias harasses a servant, who happens to be a favorite of Solomon's, by stealing half his pay and sucking out his life-force through the servant's thumb, Solomon prays for help. As a result, the archangel Michael gives him a ring with the seal of God on it. The ring gives him the power to command demons.*

*Solomon gives the ring to the servant and tells him to throw it at the demon Ornias's chest while ordering Ornias to go to Solomon.*

*Ornias tells Solomon he is the offspring of the archangel Uriel. Solomon had trouble with Ornias, so prayed that the archangel Uriel would come and help him. Uriel came from heaven and made the sea monsters come out of the deep. Uriel told the demon Ornias to cut the stones for the Temple. Solomon ordered the demon Ornias to take the ring and do the same thing to Beelzebub, the prince of demons. Beelzebub says he used to be the highest ranking angel in Heaven.*

*Solomon questions all the demons as to which angel can frustrate them.*

*The demon Error is frustrated by Uriel, as is the demon Artosael.*

*The demon Ruaz is frustrated by Michael.*

*The demon Barsafael is frustrated by Gabriel.*

*The demon Asmodeus is frustrated by Raphael, as is the demon Obizuth.*

*Solomon eventually has control over all the demons and gets them to build the Temple.*


"You have seen what Azazel has done, how he has taught every lawless act on earth, and has disclosed to the world all the secret things which are done in the heavens which humans were keen to know - also Semjaza, to whom you have given authority over his associates. They have gone together to the human women, have had sex with them, and have defiled themselves, and have revealed these crimes to them. And the women likewise have given birth to Nephilim, and so the whole earth has been filled with blood and lawlessness. And now the souls of those who are dead cry out and complain, even at heaven's portals! Their groaning ascends!

It cannot stop due to the lawlessness which is committed on earth.

"You know everything before it happens. You know these things, and what has been done by them, yet you do not tell us what we are supposed to do about it?"


**10:1-22**.

28

Then the Most High, the sacred great one spoke. He sent Uriel to Lamech's son, and said to him, "Tell him (32) in my name, 'Hide yourself!', then explain to him the event that is about to happen, that the whole earth will be destroyed, that a flooding deluge will cover the whole earth, and everything in it will be destroyed. And now tell him how he may escape, and how his descendants may remain for all generations on the earth."

Again the Lord said to Raphael, "Bind Azazel hand and foot, cast him into the darkness! Make an opening in the desert which is in Dudael, and throw him in there! Put him on rough and pointed stones, and cover him with darkness. Let him stay there forever, and cover his face so he can't see the light. And in the day of the great judgment he will be thrown into the fire. Restore the earth, which the angels have corrupted, and proclaim life to it, that they may restore it. And all the humans will not perish as a result of all the secrets of the Watchers, and which they have taught to their offspring. All the earth has been corrupted by the works that were taught by Azazel. The blame for the whole crime rests on him!"

The Lord said to Gabriel, "Go to the bastards, to the reprobates, to the offspring of immorality, and destroy them, the offspring of the Watchers, from among the humans, and send them against one another so that they will perish by killing one another, for they will not live long lives. No request their fathers make of you will be granted on their behalf. They wish to live eternally but each one of them will live for five hundred years."

The Lord said to Michael, "Go and bind Semjaza and his associates who have had sex with women and so have completely polluted and contaminated themselves! And when their sons have slain one another, and they have seen the destruction of their beloved ones, bind them for seventy generations under the earth, until the day of their judgment and of their end, until the judgment that lasts forever is completed. In those times they will be taken away to the lowest depths of the fire and tormented and they will be shut up in prison forever. Immediately after this he will, together with them, be condemned and destroyed, and they will be bound together for generation after generations."

### Punishment of the Watchers

## 2 Peter 2:4-8

*The passage in 2 Peter 2:4-8 is about the Watchers who came down to earth and rebelled against God's ordinances by whoring after human women (including those of Sodom and Gomorrah, cf. Testament of Naphtali 3.3.4-5). "God didn't spare the Messengers who sinned but handed them over to Tartarus in ropes (33) in the underworld's gloom where they are firmly held for judgment."*

## Jude

*Jude mentions the three elements that are linked in accounts of The Watchers, sorcery, going after a different flesh, and punishment of angels. Jude quotes 1 Enoch in verses 14-15:*

*"And as for the Messengers who did not uphold their own office but deserted their own places, he has held them firmly in eternal ropes down in the gloom, waiting for the Judgment of the Great Day. Just like these, Sodom and Gomorrah as well as the surrounding cities, which in a similar way committed porneia (34) and went after different flesh, (35) serve as an example of those who undergo punishment in the eternal fire."*

## Book of Jubilees 5

*The Book of Jubilees 5 sets out the punishment by God upon the Watchers and says that the flood was due to the Watchers taking human wives but that God saved Noah from it.*

*The Book of Jubilees 7:20-2 states, "Noah... encouraged his sons...to avoid porneia, uncleanness, and injustice. For it was on account of these three things that the flood came on the earth, since it was due to porneia in which the Watchers, against the regulations of their authority, had illicit sex and went a whoring after human women. When they married whomever they liked, they committed the first acts of uncleanness. They fathered as children the Nephilim."*

*"And he testified about the Watchers, who had sinned with the female humans, for they had begun to sleep with the female humans causing defilement, and Enoch testified against them all." (Jubilees 4:22)*

*"It happened when the humans began to increase on the face of the earth and daughters were born to them, that the angels of God saw them on a certain year of this jubilee, and saw that they were beautiful to look at, and they chose wives, anyone they wanted,*

*and the wives bore them children and they were Nephilim. Lawlessness increased on the earth and everything of the earthly realm became corrupt, humans, cattle, wild animals, birds, and everything that walked on the earth - all of them corrupted their ways and their orders, and they began to eat each other.*

*Lawlessness increased on the earth and every imagination of all human thought was continually evil. And God looked at the earth, and saw it was corrupt, and everything of the earthly realm had corrupted its order, and all that were on the earth had done all kinds of evil in front of his eyes. He said: "I will destroy humans and all living things on the face of the earth that I created."*
*(Jubilees 5:1-4)*

### Testament of Naphtali 3.3.4-5

*The Testament of Naphtali 3.3.4-5 states that the women of Sodom had sex with the Watchers. It states, "In the same way also the Watchers changed the order of their nature. The Lord cursed the Watchers at the flood, and made the earth desolate because of them, so that it would be uninhabited and fruitless." Note the term "changed the order of their nature" which is similar to Jude's term, "went after different flesh" and to Paul's statement, "for the females exchanged natural sex for what is other than nature. And the same goes for males too," in Romans 1:26.*

### The Church Father Irenaeus

*The Church Father Irenaeus stated, "And wickedness very long-continued and widespread pervaded all the races of men, until very little seed of justice was in them. For unlawful unions came about on earth, as angels linked themselves with offspring of the daughters of men, who bore to them sons, who on account of their exceeding great were called Giants. The angels, then, brought to their wives as gifts teachings of evil, for they taught them the virtues of roots and herbs, and dyeing and cosmetics and discoveries of precious materials, love-philtes, hatreds, amours, passions, constraints of love, the bonds of witchcraft, every sorcery and idolatry, hateful to God, and when this was come into the world, the affairs of wickedness were propagated to overflowing, and those of justice dwindled to very little."*

*(Irenaeus, Demonstration, 18. Joseph P. Smith, St. Irenaeus: Proof of the Apostolic Preaching, London, 1952, p. 58.)*

### The second century theologian Tatian

*The second century theologian Tatian, 2 Apology 5, stated, "God committed the care of humans and everything under heaven to angels whom he appointed over them. But the angels disobeyed this appointment, and were captivated by the love of women. They produced children who are called demons, and not only that, they later subjugated the human race for themselves, partly by magical writings, partly by fears and the punishments they brought about, and partly by teaching them to offer sacrifices, incense, and libations, as they needed these things after they were enslaved by lust. Among humankind they sowed murders, wars, adulteries, awful actions, and all kinds of wickedness."*

### Clement of Alexandria

*Clement of Alexandria, Miscellanies 5.1.10 stated, "To this we will also add, that the angels who had obtained the superior rank, after sinking into pleasures, told the women the secrets which had come to their knowledge."*

### 2 Enoch

*2 Enoch 10: "1 Those two men led me up on to the north side, and showed me there an awful place. There were all kinds of tortures in that place, brutal darkness and the gloom of darkness. There is no light there, but a gloomy fire constantly burning high, and a fiery river coming out. The whole place is on fire, and everywhere there is frost, ice, thirst, and cold. The bonds are very cruel, and the angels frightening and without compassion. They carry fierce weapons and harsh torture. I said, 2 "Woe, woe, this place is so awful!" 3 And those men replied, "Enoch, this place is prepared for those who dishonor God, who on earth practice crime against nature, child-corruption, magic-making, enchantments, and devilish witchcrafts, and who boast of their wicked deeds, stealing, lies, slander, envy, resentment, porneia, murder. They are accursed and steal people's lives, and take away the possessions of the poor in order to make themselves rich, harming them, and although they are able to feed the hungry, make them starve to death, and although they can clothe people, they strip them naked. They did not acknowledge their creator, and bowed down to the soulless and lifeless gods who cannot see nor hear, useless gods, and they also built carved images and bowed down to unclean work. This whole place is prepared for their eternal inheritance."*

Destroy all the lustful spirits, and the offspring of the Watchers, for they have committed crimes against humankind. Let all oppressors perish from the face of the earth and let every evil work be destroyed. Let the plant of justice and truth appear and become a blessing. Justice and truth will be forever planted with enjoyment. And then all the devoted people will be thankful, and live until they have produced a thousand children, while the whole time of their youth, and their old age, will come to an end peacefully

In those times the whole earth will be cultivated with justice, and will be planted with trees and be filled with blessings. And all desirable trees will be planted on it. They will plant vines on it. The vines which they plant will yield abundant wine. Every seed which is sown on it will produce a thousand measures for one measure, and produce ten presses of oil for one measure of olives.

Cleanse the earth from all oppression, from all injustice, from all crimes, from all godlessness, and from all the pollution which is committed on it. Eliminate them from the earth. Then all the humans will be just, and all nations will highly respect me and bless me, and all will esteem me. The earth will be cleansed from all defilement, from every crime, from all punishment, and from all torment, and I will never again send torment on it for generation after generation, forever.

## 11:1-2.

In those days I will open the storehouses of blessing which are in heaven, so as to make them descend on earth over all the work and labor of humankind. Peace and fair play will associate with humankind for all the days of the world, in every generation.

## 12:1-6.

Before all these things, Enoch was hidden, and none of the humans knew where he was hidden, where he had been, and what had happened. His days were with the sacred ones, and his doings were to do with the Watchers.

I, Enoch, was blessing the great Lord and King of ages, when the Watchers called me - Enoch the scribe - and said to me, "Enoch, you just scribe of justice, go and tell the Watchers of heaven, who have deserted the high heaven, the sacred everlasting place, who have been defiled with women and have done as the humans do, by taking wives for themselves, 'You have greatly caused corruption on the earth. You will never have peace or forgiveness for your crimes. You will have no delight in your offspring, for you will see the slaughter of their loved ones, and you will lament for the destruction of your children. You can make petition forever, but you will not obtain compassion or peace!'"

## 13:1-10.

Then Enoch went on and said to Azazel, "You will not find peace. A severe sentence has gone out against you, that you are to be bound. You will find no relief, compassion, or granting of requests, because of the injustice you have taught, because of every act of blasphemy, lawlessness, and wrongdoing, which you have shown to humankind."

Then I left him and spoke to them all together, and they were terrified, seized with fear and trembling. They asked me to write a petition for them so that they might find forgiveness, and for me to read their petition in the presence of the Lord of heaven, because from then on they could not address him, or lift up their eyes to heaven on account of the appalling offence for which they were judged.

Then I wrote out their petition and the prayer for their spirits, for everything which they had done, and in regard to their requests, that they should have forgiveness and rest. Then I continued on and sat down at the waters of Dan, in the land of Dan, to the right of the west of Hermon. I read their petition until I fell asleep.

And a dream came to me, and visions fell on me. I saw visions of punishment, so that I might relate it to the heavenly ones, and reprimand them. When I awoke I went to them. They were all sitting gathered together in Abelsjail, which is situated between Lebanon and Seneser, (_36_) crying, with their faces covered. I related in their presence all the visions which I had seen, and my dream. And I began to utter the just words of justice, reprimanding the heavenly Watchers.

## 14:1-25.

This is the book of the just words, and of the reprimand of the Watchers, who are from eternity, according to what the sacred and great one commanded in the vision. I saw in my dream, what I will now speak with a tongue of flesh, and my breath, which the Mighty One has given to the human mouth to converse with and to understand with the heart. As he has created and given to humans the power of comprehending the word of understanding, so has he created and given to me the power of reprimanding the Watchers, the heavenly ones.

"I have written your petition, and in my vision it appeared to me, that what you request will not be granted to you as long as the world lasts. Judgment has been passed on you: your request will not be granted to you. From this time forward, you will not ascend into heaven for all eternity, and he has said that you will be bound on the earth as long as the world lasts. And before these things, you will see the destruction of your loved offspring. You will not have them, but they will fall in front of you by the sword. Your petition on their behalf will not be granted, nor for yourselves, despite your crying and praying and speaking all the words in the writing which I have written."

A vision appeared to me. In that vision clouds and a mist invited me. The pathway of the stars and flashes of lightning summoned me and pressed me forwards, while the winds in the vision caused me to fly, speeding up my progress, and lifted me to heaven. I continued until I arrived at a wall built with crystals and surrounded by tongues of fire which began to terrify me.

I went into the tongues of fire and drew close to a large dwelling also built with crystals. Its walls and pavement were made with crystals, and the ground was also crystal. Its roof was like the path of the stars and flashes of lightning, and among them were fiery cherubs (37) in a watery sky. A flaming fire surrounded the walls, and its doorway blazed with fire. When I entered the dwelling, it was as hot as fire and cold as ice. There was no trace of delight or of life there. Terror seized me, and a dread shaking seized me.

Violently disconcerted and trembling, I fell on my face. In the vision I saw another dwelling bigger than the former. Every entrance to it stood open in front of me. It was built of fiery flames. In every way it so excelled in splendor and magnificence and size that it is impossible to describe to you either the splendor or the extent of it. Its floor was on fire and above it were flashes of lightning and the path of the stars. Its roof was flaming fire.

I looked and saw that it contained a high throne, the appearance of which was like a crystal, while its circumference resembled the brilliant sun, and there was the voice of the cherubs.

From underneath the throne came rivers of flaming fire. To look on it was impossible. The splendid one sat on it. His robe was brighter than the sun, and whiter than snow. No angel could enter and look at his face because of the splendor and grandeur, nor could any mortal look at him. The flaming fire was around him. A huge fire also continued to rise up in front of him and no one who surrounded him was able to approach him, among the myriads of myriads who were in front of him. He needed no counselor. The most sacred ones who were near him did not leave him by night or by day, nor did they go far from him. Until then I had been on my face, and trembling. Then the Lord called me with his own mouth and said, "Come here, Enoch, and hear my word."

He made me rise up and approach the entrance. My face was directed to the ground.

## 15:1-12.

Then he answered me, and I heard his voice. He said, "Don't be afraid, Enoch, you are a just scribe of justice. Approach, and hear my voice. Go, and say to the heavenly Watchers, who have sent you to pray for them, 'You ought to pray for humans, and not humans for you. You have left the high and sacred heaven, which lasts for ever, and have slept with women. You have defiled yourselves with the human women and have taken wives, you have acted like the humans, and you have produced Nephilim as your offspring!

"And although you were sacred, spiritual, and possessing eternal life, you have defiled yourselves with the blood of women, have produced with the blood of the natural realm, have lusted like humans and have done as those who are flesh and blood do. These however die and perish. Therefore have I given them wives, that they might get them pregnant and produce children with them, and that this might be conducted on the earth. But you from the beginning were made spiritual, having eternal life, immortal for all generations. Therefore I did not make wives for you, because, being spiritual, your dwelling is in heaven.

"Now the Nephilim, who are produced from spirit and flesh, will be called on earth evil spirits, and they will live on earth. Evil spirits have proceeded from their bodies, because they were created from humans: from the sacred Watchers was their beginning and primary origin. Evil spirits they will be on earth, and the spirits of the wicked they will be called.

"As for the spirits of heaven, they will live in heaven, but as for the spirits of the earth which were born on the earth, they will live on the earth. The spirits of the Nephilim will oppress, afflict, destroy, do battle, and bruise on the earth. They will cause grief. They will not eat food, and they will be thirsty, they will cause trouble. They will (_38_) rise up against the humans, and against women, because they have proceeded from them."

### Account in the Book of Jubilees

*The Book of Jubilees says that only one-tenth of evil spirits will be allowed to harm humans.*

*"'And you know how your Watchers, the fathers of these spirits, acted in my day. And as for these spirits which are living, imprison them and bind them in the place of condemnation, and do not let them bring destruction on the children of your servant, my God, because they are evil, and created in order to destroy. Do not let them rule over the spirits of the living, for you alone can rule over them. Do not let them have power over the just from now on and for evermore.'*

*"And the Lord our God told us to bind them all. The chief of the spirits, Mastema, came and said, 'Lord, Creator, let some of them stay with me, and let them do as I say, and do everything I tell them to do, because if some of them are not left for me, I will not be able to do what I want with the humans, and they are bent on fraud and being led astray in my judgment, for the wickedness of the humans is immense.' God said, 'Let a tenth of them stay with him, and let*

37

*the other nine parts descend into the place of condemnation.' He
commanded one of us to teach Noah all their medicines, for he
knew that they would not behave with integrity or justice. So we did
what he said: all the nasty evil ones we bound in the place of
condemnation, and we left a tenth of them to be subject to
Adversary on the earth. We explained to Noah all the medicines for
their diseases, and how they worked, and how to heal them with
herbs of the earth. Noah wrote down everything we instructed him
about every kind of medicine in a book. Thus the evil spirits were
prevented from doing anything to Noah's children."*

## 16:1-4.

"During the days of slaughter and destruction of the Nephilim,
whenever their spirits depart from their bodies, their flesh will be
destroyed before the judgment. Thus they will perish, until the day
of the great end of the great world. A destruction will take place of
the Watchers and the wicked. And now as for the Watchers, who
have sent you to pray for them, who previously were in heaven, say
to them, 'You have been in heaven, but all the mysteries had not
been revealed to you. You knew worthless ones, and because of
your stubbornness you have related these to the women, and
through these mysteries women and humankind have done much
evil on the earth. Say to them, 'You will never obtain peace!'"

## Enoch's travels through the Earth and through Sheol

## 17:1-8.

They took me to a certain place, and those who were there were like
flaming fire, and when they wished to, they assumed the appearance
of humans. They carried me to the place of darkness, to a mountain,
the top of which reached heaven. And I saw the receptacles of the
luminaries and of thunder at the uttermost extremities, where it was
deepest. There was a fiery bow, and arrows in their quiver, a fiery
sword, and every type of lightning.

Then they took me to living water, and to a fire in the west, which
received every setting of the sun. I came to a river of fire, which
flowed like water, and emptied itself into the great sea towards the

west. I saw every large river, until I arrived at the great darkness. I went to the place where no flesh walks. I saw the mountains of the gloom of winter, and the place from which the water of every abyss flows. I saw the mouths of all the rivers in the world, and the mouth of the deep.

## 18:1-16.

I then saw the holders of all the winds. I saw how they contributed to the whole creation and the foundations of the earth. I saw the cornerstone of the earth. I also saw the four winds, which bear up the earth, and the structure of the sky. And I saw the winds occupying the high sky, being in the midst of heaven and of earth, and constituting the pillars of heaven.

I saw the winds of the sky, which turn and cause the orb of the sun and of all the stars to set, and over the earth I saw the winds carrying the clouds. I saw the paths of the angels. I saw the structure of the sky above at the extremity of the earth. Then I headed south, and saw a place which burns day and night, where there are seven mountains formed of superb stones, three towards the east, and three towards the south. Of those which were towards the east, one was a colored stone, one was of pearl, and another of healing stone. Those towards the south were of a red stone.

The middle one reached to heaven like God's throne. It was of alabaster, and the top was of sapphire. I also saw blazing fire. Over all the mountains is a place on the other side of a large territory, where waters were collected. I also saw a deep abyss, with columns of heavenly fire. And in the heavenly columns I saw fires, which were beyond measure both as regards their height and depth. Over this abyss I also saw a place which did not have the structure of the sky above it, nor the solid ground underneath it. There was no water above it, nor any birds, but it was a desolate place. And there I saw seven stars, like great blazing mountains, and like spirits entreating me.

There I saw seven stars like great burning mountains, and when I inquired about them, the angel said, "This place is the end of heaven and earth: this has become a prison for the stars and the host of heaven. The stars which roll over the fire are those which disobeyed the Lord's instruction in the beginning of their time, because they did not come at their appointed times. Therefore he was angry with them, and bound them until the time when their sentence would be completed, in ten thousand years."

## 19:1-3.

Then Uriel said to me, "The angels who were promiscuous with women will stand here. Their spirits will assume many different forms. They will defile humankind and lead them astray into sacrificing to demons as gods. They will stand here until the great day of judgment, in which they will be judged, until they are made an end of. But their wives who led astray the angels of heaven will find peace."

And I, Enoch, alone saw the vision of the end of all things. No other human saw what I saw.

## The Watchers who did not fall

## 20:1-8.

These are the names of the sacred angels who watch. Uriel, one of the sacred angels, who presides over the world and Tartarus.

### *Tartarus*

*The Greeks considered Hades to be the underworld, full of ghosts or wraiths of people who had died. Homer's Odyssey speaks of Odysseus raising spirits from Hades and notes that these spirits could be strengthened when they drank blood. It also speaks of people continuing their earthly ways – for example, one person was professionally hunting. It was spoken of as a terrifying, eerie place, but not specifically a place of punishment like Tartarus. Hades is commonly translated as "Hell" in most Bible versions, as are "Gehenna" and "Tartarus," yet to the Greeks, they were separate places. Tartarus was the lowest region of the underworld, said to be as far below Hades as the earth is under the sky. Tartarus was the place where the very wicked were punished. The Greeks believed Hades to be midway between heaven and Tartarus. See Aeschylus, Prom. 152-6: "Would that he had hurled me underneath the earth and*

*underneath the House of Hades, host to the dead – yes, down to*
*limitless Tartarus, yes, though he bound me cruelly in chains*
*breakable."*

*(Trans. David Grene.)*

*The Septuagint translated Sheol as "Hades."*

Raphael, one of the sacred angels, who is over human spirits.
Raguel, one of the sacred angels, who inflicts punishment on the
world and the luminaries. Michael, one of the sacred angels who is
over the most part of humankind, in charge of the nations. Saraqael,
one of the sacred angels, who presides over the spirits of the
humans that do wrong. Gabriel, one of the sacred angels, who
presides over the seraphim, (*39*) over paradise, (*40*) and over the
cherubim.

Remiel, one of the sacred angels, whom God set over those who rise.


### Enoch's second journey


**21:1-10.**

Then I went to a place where things were dreadful. There I saw
neither a high heaven nor an established earth, but a desolate
appalling spot. There I saw seven stars of heaven bound together in
it, like great mountains of blazing fire. I said, "For what type of
crime have they been bound, and why have they been thrown into
this place?"

Then Uriel, one of the sacred angels who was with me, and who
guided me, answered, "Enoch, why do you ask, why do you
earnestly inquire? These are those of the stars which have
disobeyed the Lord's commandment, and are bound here until ten
thousand years, the time of their crimes, have come to pass."

Afterwards I went on from there to another dreadful place, more
ghastly than the former, where I saw a huge blazing and glittering
fire, in the middle of which there was a split as far as the abyss. It
was full of huge columns of fire, and their descent was deep. I could
not discover its measurement or magnitude, nor could I perceive its

source. Then I exclaimed, "How horrifying this place is, and how difficult to explore!"

Then Uriel, one of the sacred angels who was with me, answered me, "Enoch, why are you alarmed and amazed at this appalling place, at the sight of this place of pain?" He told me, "This is the prison of the angels, and they are kept here for ever."

## 22:1-14.

From there I went to another spot, and he showed me an immense high mountain of hard rock in the west. There were four hollow places in it which were deep and very smooth. Three of them were dark and one was bright, and there was a fountain of water in the middle of it. I said, "These beautiful places are so smooth, and so and deep and dark to look at!"

Then Raphael, one of the sacred angels who was with me, answered, "The beautiful places have been created for this very purpose, for the spirits of the souls of the dead to assemble in them, so that all the souls of humans should assemble here. They will stay in these places until the day of their judgment, until their appointed time. Their appointed time will be long, until the great judgment."

And I saw the spirits of humans who were dead, and their voices reached heaven in complaint. Then I asked Raphael, the angel who was with me, "Whose spirit is that, the voice of which reaches to heaven in complaint?"

He answered me, "This is the spirit of Abel who was slain by his brother Cain, and who will accuse that brother, until his descendants are wiped off the face of the earth, until his descendants are annihilated from the descendants of the human race."

At that time I asked about him, and about the general judgment, "Why is one separated from another?"

He answered, "These three have been made so that the spirits of the dead might be separated. This division has been made for the spirits of the just, in which there is the bright spring of water. And this has been made for wrongdoers when they die and are buried in the earth when judgment has not been executed on them in their lifetime. Here their spirits will be separated in this great pain, until the time of the great judgment, the scoldings, and the torments of the accursed, whose souls are punished and bound there for ever. Thus has it been from the beginning of the world.

"And this division has been made for the spirits of those who make complaints, who give information about their destruction, when they were killed in the days of the wrongdoers. This has been made for the spirits of unjust humans who are wrongdoers, those who have committed crimes, and are godless associates of the lawless. But their spirits will not be annihilated in the day of judgment, nor will they arise from this place."

Then I blessed the splendid Lord, "Blessed are you, just Lord, who reigns over everything for ever and ever!"

## 23:1-4.

From there I went to another place, towards the west, to the extremities of the earth. There I saw a blazing fire which ran without ceasing, and did not change its course day or night, but always continued the same.

I asked, "What is this, which doesn't cease?"

Then Raguel, one of the sacred angels who was with me, answered, "This blazing fire, which you see running towards the west, is the fire of all the heavenly luminaries."

### The Fragrant Trees

## 24:1-7.

I went from there to another place, and saw a mountain of fire which burned day and night. I went past it, and saw seven impressive mountains, which were all different from each other.

Their stones were dazzling and beautiful, all were brilliant and splendid to look at, and their surface was attractive. Three mountains were towards the east, and one placed on the other, and three were towards the south, one placed on the other. There were deep ravines, which did not join each other. The seventh mountain was in the middle of them and was taller, resembling the seat of a throne, and fragrant trees surrounded it.

Among these there was a tree such as I have never smelled. None of the others there were like it. It had a fragrance beyond all other fragrances. Its leaf, its flower, and its bark never withered, and its fruit was beautiful. Its fruit resembled the cluster of the palm. I exclaimed, "This tree is beautiful! Its leaves are gorgeous, and its fruit is a delight to the eye!"

Then Michael, one of the sacred splendid angels who was with me, and was their leader,

## 25:1-7.

responded, "Enoch, why do you inquire about the fragrance of this tree? Why are you inquisitive to know about it?"

Then I answered him, "I would like to know everything, but particularly about this tree."

He answered me, "That mountain which you saw, whose summit resembles God's throne, will be the seat on which the sacred and great splendid Lord, the everlasting king, will sit when he comes down to visit the earth for the good. And as for that perfumed tree of an agreeable smell, no mortal is permitted to touch it, until the time of the great judgment, when he will punish all and bring everything to an end forever. It will be then be given to the just and sacred. Its fruit will be food for the chosen. It will be transplanted to the sacred place, by the house of the Lord, the everlasting king. Then will they celebrate greatly and be happy. They will enter the scared place and its fragrance will enter their bones. They will live a long life on the earth as your ancestors lived. No sorrow, plague, trouble, or tragedy will touch them."

Then I blessed the splendid Lord, the everlasting king, because he has prepared this tree for the just ones, and declared that he would give it to them.

## 26:1-6.

From there I went to the middle of the earth, and saw a blessed fertile spot, which contained branches continually sprouting from the trees which were planted in it. There I saw a sacred mountain, and underneath the mountain to the east there was a stream which flowed towards the south. I also saw to the east another mountain higher than it, and between them was a deep, narrow ravine. A stream ran under the mountain. To the west was another mountain, lower and smaller, and a deep and dry ravine ran between them. In the middle of them was another deep and dry ravine at the extremities of the three mountains. All these ravines, which were deep and narrow, and formed of hard rock, had no trees planted on them. And I was in awe of the rock and of the ravine; I was very much in awe.

## 27:1-4.

Then I said, "What is the purpose of this blessed land, which is full of trees, and the accursed valley between them?"

Then Uriel, one of the sacred angels with me, replied, "This valley is for those who are accursed for ever. Here all those who speak inappropriate language against the Lord, and speak harsh things about his splendor will be collected. Here will they be collected, here will be their territory. In the last times, in the time of judgment in the presence of the just ones, those who have received compassion will bless the splendid Lord, the everlasting king, for all their days, forever. In the time of judgment they will bless him for his compassion, as he has assigned it to them." Then I blessed the splendid Lord, addressing him, and making mention of his greatness.

## 28:1-2.

From there I headed east to the middle of the mountain range in the desert, and saw a wilderness, full of trees and plants, and water gushed down on it. A cascade of water appeared there. It was composed of many cascades of water both to the west and the east. On one side were trees, and on the other side were water and dew. The watercourse rushed to the northwest causing clouds and spray to go up on all sides.

## 29:1-2.

Then I went to another place in the desert, and approached the east of that mountain range. There I saw first rate trees, those which produce frankincense and myrrh, and the trees were not alike.

## 30:1-3.

And beyond them, I went to the east and saw another place with valleys full of water. In there was a tree, the color of the fragrant trees such as the mastic. And on the sides of these valleys I saw sweetly smelling cinnamon. Past these I advanced towards the east.

## 31:1-3.

Then I saw other mountains containing trees, from which water flowed like nectar called sarara and galbanum. And beyond these mountains I saw another mountain, and the trees were full of fruit like a hard almond. This fruit smelt sweeter than any fragrance.

## 32:1-6.

After these things I saw the entrances of the north east and saw seven mountains full of first-rate nard, mastic, cinnamon, and pepper. From there I passed on above the summits of those mountains to some distance eastwards, and went over the Erythraean Sea. When I had gone far beyond it, I passed along above the angel Zotiel, and arrived at the garden of justice. There I saw from afar off, trees more numerous and greater than these trees. They were sweet smelling, large, fine-looking and elegant. The tree of knowledge was there. If any one eats from it, they gain great wisdom.

It was like the carob tree, bearing fruit which resembled very fine grapes, and its perfume extended a great distance. I exclaimed, "How beautiful is this tree, and how delightful is its appearance!"

Then the sacred angel Raphael who was with me, responded, "This is the tree of wisdom, of which your ancient father and your ancient mother ate, who came before you, and they obtained wisdom and their eyes were opened, and then they knew that they were naked, and were expelled from the garden."

## 33:1-4.

From there I went on towards the extremities of the earth, where I saw large beasts different from each other, and birds also differing in appearance, beauty and voice, different from each other. To the east of these beasts I saw the extremities of the earth, where heaven rests, and the portals of heaven stood open. I saw the celestial stars come out. I counted them as they proceeded out of the portal, and wrote them all down, as they came out one by one according to their number and their names, their times and their seasons, as the angel Uriel, who was with me, pointed them out to me. He showed them all to me, and wrote them down for me. He also wrote down for me their names, their regulations, and their operations.

## 34:1-3.

From there I went towards the north, to the extremities of the earth. There I saw a great and glorious wonder at the extremities of the whole earth. There I saw three heavenly portals open, and the north winds proceed from them, blowing cold, hail, frost, snow, dew, and rain. From one of the portals they blew mildly, but when they blew from the two other portals, it was with violence and force. They blew over the earth strongly.

## 35:1.

From there I went to the west to the extremities of the earth and there I saw three heavenly portals such as I had seen in the east, the same number of portals, and the same number of passages.

## 36:1-4.

From there I went south to the extremities of the earth, where I saw three heavenly open portals, from which issued dew, rain, and wind. From there I went east to the extremities of heaven, where I saw three eastern heavenly portals open, and these had smaller portals within them. Through each of these small portals the stars of heaven pass west by a path which is shown to them.

Every time they appeared, I blessed the splendid Lord, who had made those great splendid signs, in order to display the magnificence of his works to angels and to spirits and to humans, so that these would praise all his works and operations, would see his powerful works, and would praise his amazing labor, and bless him for ever.

# The Parables

## 37:1-5.

The second vision he saw, the vision of wisdom, which Enoch, the son of Jared, the son of Mahalalel, the son of Cainan, the son of Enos, the son of Seth, the son of Adam, saw. This is the start of the word of wisdom, which I received to declare and tell to those who live on earth. Listen, you people of old, see, and you who come after, from the beginning, and understand to the end, the words of the sacred one which I will speak in the presence of the Lord of spirits. It would have been better to declare them only to the people of old, but we will not withhold the beginning of wisdom from those who come after. Until the present time there never has been such wisdom given by the Lord of spirits as that which I have received, wisdom according to my insight, according to the wish of the Lord of spirits, by whom the portion of eternal life has been given to me. And I obtained three parables, and I lifted up my voice and told them to the inhabitants of the earth.

## The First Parable

## 38:1-6.

### The first parable.

When the congregation of the just appears, and wrongdoers are judged for their crimes, and are driven from the face of the earth.

When the just one appears (*41*) in the presence of the just themselves, who will be elected for their good works duly weighed by the Lord of spirits, and when the light appears to the just and the chosen ones, who live on earth, where will the dwelling of wrongdoers be? And where will be the place of rest for those who have rejected the Lord of spirits? It would have been better for them if had they never been born.

When the secrets of the just will be revealed and the wrongdoers judged, and the impious driven from the presence of the just and the chosen, from that time those who possess the earth will cease to be powerful and exalted. They will not be able to look at the faces of the sacred, for the Lord of spirits has made his light appear on the faces of the sacred, the just, and the chosen. The mighty kings of that time will be destroyed and delivered to the hands of the just and sacred. From then on no one will attain compassion from the Lord of spirits, because their lives will be at an end.

## 39:1-13.

In those days the chosen and sacred race will descend from the upper heavens, and their offspring will become one with the humans. In those days Enoch received books of indignation and anger, and books of agitation and confusion.

"They will never obtain compassion," says the Lord of spirits.

In those days a whirlwind snatched me up, and raised me above the earth's surface, setting me down at the extremity of the heavens.

There I saw another vision. I saw the dwellings and resting places of the sacred ones and the resting places of the just. There my eyes saw their dwellings with the sacred ones. They were entreating, interceding, and praying for the humans. Justice flowed in front of them like water, and compassion was scattered over the earth like dew. And so it will be with them for ever and for ever.

At that time my eyes saw the dwelling of the chosen ones of truth, faith, and justice. There will be justice in their days, and the just and chosen ones will be without number, in his presence, for ever and ever. I saw his dwelling under the wings of the Lord of spirits. All the sacred and the chosen ones sang in his presence looking like a blazing fire. Their mouths were full of blessings, and their lips were praising the name of the Lord of spirits. And justice was always before him.

I wished to stay there, and my inner self longed for that dwelling. There my allotment had been previously assigned to me in the presence of the Lord of Spirits.

In those times I praised and extolled the name of the Lord of spirits with blessings and praises, for he has destined me with blessing and favor, according to his own good pleasure. My eyes contemplated that place for a long time. I blessed him and said, "May he be blessed, blessed from the beginning and forever!"

In his presence there is no end. He knew before the world was created what the world would become, for generation after

49

generation. Those who do not sleep bless you. They stand in the presence of your splendor and bless, praise, and exalt you, saying, "The sacred, sacred, sacred Lord of spirits fills the earth with spirits."

There my eyes saw all who do not sleep and stand in his presence and bless him, saying, "May you be blessed, may the name of God be blessed for ever and for ever!"

Then my face became changed until I was incapable of seeing.


## 40:1-9.

After this I saw thousands of thousands, and ten thousand times ten thousand, and an infinite number of people, standing in front of the Lord of spirits. On the four sides of the Lord of spirits, I saw four figures, different from those who were standing before him and I learnt their names, because the angel, who went with me, told them to me, and showed me every secret thing.

Then I heard the voices of the four figures praising the splendid Lord. The first voice blessed the Lord of spirits for ever and ever.

I heard the second voice blessing the chosen one, and the chosen ones who rely on the Lord of spirits. I heard the third voice interceding and praying for those who live on earth, and requesting in the name of the Lord of spirits.

I heard the fourth voice expelling the satans, (42) and prohibiting them from entering the presence of the Lord of spirits to accuse the inhabitants of the earth.

After that I asked the angel of peace who went with me, to explain everything that is hidden. I asked, "Who are the four figures I have seen, whose words have I heard and written down?"

He replied, "The first is the merciful, patient, and sacred Michael.

The second is the sacred Raphael, who is set over all diseases and afflictions of humans. The third is Gabriel, who is set over all the powers. And the fourth is Phanuel, who is set over repentance, and the hope of those who will inherit eternal life." These are the four angels of the Lord of spirits, and their four voices, which I heard in those times.

**41:1-9.**

After this I saw the secrets of the heavens and how the kingdom is divided, and how human action is weighed there in the balances. I saw the dwellings of the chosen ones, and the dwellings of the sacred ones. And there my eyes saw all the wrongdoers who denied the Lord of spirits, being dragged away, as they could not stay because of the punishment proceeding against them from the Lord of spirits.

There, too, my eyes saw the secrets of the lightning and the thunder, and the secrets of the winds, how they are distributed as they blow over the earth, and the secrets of the clouds and dew. There I saw the place from which they issued, and from where they saturate the earth's dust. There I saw the closed containers, out of which the winds are distributed, the container of hail, the container of snow, the container of the clouds, and the cloud itself, which remained over the earth before the creation of the world.

I saw also the containers of the sun and moon, where they come from, and where they go to, their glorious return, and how one became more splendid than the other. I marked their majestic course, their unchangeable course, how they do not add or subtract anything to their course, and how they keep faith in each other by their stable oath. The sun goes out first and completes its course in accordance with the commandment of the Lord of spirits; his name is powerful for ever and ever!

After this I saw the path, both concealed and apparent, of the moon, and how the moon's path progresses by day and by night. One stands opposite the other in front of the Lord of spirits, honoring and praising without ceasing, since praising is like a rest to them.

For the splendid sun makes many revolutions both for a blessing and a curse. The course of the moon's path is light for the just, but darkness for the wrongdoers. In the name of the Lord, who made a division between light and darkness, and divided the spirits of humans, and strengthened the spirits of the righteous in the name of his justice. No angel hinders this, and no power is able to hinder it, because the judge sees them all, and judges them all in his own presence.

**42:1-3.**

51

Wisdom found no place on earth where she could live, and her dwelling was in heaven. Wisdom went out to live among the humans, but did not find a place to live. Wisdom returned to her place, and took her seat in the midst of the angels. But wickedness went out of her chambers. She found those she did not seek, and lived among them, like rain in the desert and on a thirsty land.

## 43:1-4.

I saw flashes of lightning and the stars of heaven. I saw that he called them all by their names, and that they heard. I saw that he weighed them with a just balance, according to their light, according to the width of their areas and the day of their appearance and how their revolution produces lightning. I saw their revolutions, according to the number of the angels, and how they keep faith with each other.

I asked the angel who went with me, and explained secret things to me, "What are their names?"

He answered, "The Lord of spirits has shown you their parable. They are the names of the sacred ones who live on earth, and who believe the name of the Lord of spirits for ever and ever."

## 44:1.

I saw other things with regard to the lightning - how some of the stars rise and become lightning but cannot lose their form.

## The Second Parable

### 45:1-6.

This is the second parable, about those who deny the name and the dwelling of the sacred ones, and of the Lord of spirits. They will not ascend to heaven, nor will they come to the earth. This will be the fate of wrongdoers, who deny the name of the Lord of spirits, and who are reserved for the day of punishment and affliction.

On that day the chosen one will sit on a splendid throne, and will consider their actions, and they will have countless resting places. Their inner selves will be strengthened, when they see my chosen one, and those who have called on my sacred, splendid name. At that time I will cause my chosen one to live amongst them, and I will change the face of heaven and make it a blessing and a light forever. I will also change the face of the earth and make it a blessing, and cause my chosen ones to live on it. But those who have committed wrongdoing and wickedness will not live on it. I have taken note and satisfied my just ones with peace, and placed them in my presence, but as for the wrongdoers, their judgment will draw near so that I may destroy them from the face of the earth.

**46:1-8.**

There I saw the Ancient of Days, whose head was like white wool, and with him another, whose appearance looked like a human's. His appearance was very elegant, like one of the sacred angels. And I asked the angel who went with me, and explained secret things to me, about that human, who he was, and where did he come from, and why did he go with the Ancient of Days.

He answered me, "This is the human, to whom justice belongs, and with whom justice lives. He will reveal all the treasures of that which is hidden, for the Lord of spirits has chosen him, and because of his justice, his share has surpassed all others in the presence of the Lord of spirits forever.

"This human, who you have seen, will stir up kings and the powerful from their dwellings, and the strong from their thrones, will loosen the reins of the strong, and break the teeth of the wrongdoers. He will throw kings from their thrones and their kingdoms, because they do not exalt and praise him, and do not respectfully acknowledge the source by which their kingdoms were granted to them. He will throw down the appearance of the strong and fill them with shame. Darkness will be their dwelling, and worms will be their bed. They will have no hope of being raised from their bed, because they have not praised the name of the Lord of spirits.

"They will judge the stars of heaven, and will lift up their hands against the Most High. They will tread on and inhabit the earth, exhibiting all their wicked actions. Their power rests on their wealth, and their faith is in the gods whom they have formed with their own hands. They deny the name of the Lord of spirits, and will expel him from his assembly places, and with him the faithful, who depend on the name of the Lord of spirits."

## 47:1-4.

In those days the prayer of the sacred and the blood of the just will ascend from the earth into the presence of the Lord of spirits. In those days the sacred ones, who live above the heavens, will unite with one voice, and petition, pray, praise, extol, and bless the name of the Lord of spirits, because of the blood of the just which has been shed, and so that the prayer of the just will not be in vain in the presence of the Lord of spirits, and so that justice may be done for them, and so that they don't have to wait patiently forever.

In those days, I saw the Ancient of Days while he sat on his splendid throne, and the books of the living were opened in his presence, while his entire host in the heavens above and his council stood around in his presence. The hearts of the sacred ones were very happy that the number of the just had been reached, and that the prayer of the just had been heard, and that the blood of the just had not been required in the presence of the Lord of spirits.

## 48:1-10.

In that place I saw a spring of justice which never ceased, surrounded by many springs of wisdom. All the thirsty drank from them, and were filled with wisdom, and their dwelling was with the honest, the chosen, and the sacred. At that hour that human was called in the presence of the Lord of spirits, and his name brought into the presence of the Ancient of Days.

Before the sun and the signs were created, before the stars of heaven were formed, his name was called in the presence of the Lord of spirits. He will be a support for the just and the sacred to lean on and not fall, and he will be a light to the nations. He will be the hope of those whose hearts are troubled. All who live on earth will fall down and worship him and will bless and praise him, and sing praise songs celebrating the name of the Lord of spirits. Therefore he has been chosen and hidden in his presence, before the world was created, and forever. But the wisdom of the Lord of spirits has revealed him to the sacred and the honest, for he has kept the share belonging to the just ones safe, because they have hated and rejected this world of wickedness, and have detested all its works and ways, in the name of the Lord of spirits. For they are saved by his name, and his wishes will be their life.

In those days the kings of the earth and the strong, who possess the land by their achievements, will have downcast faces. For in the day of their anguish and trouble they will not be able to save themselves, and I will hand them over to my chosen ones. Like hay in the fire, they will burn in the presence of the honest, and like lead in the water, they will sink in the presence of the sacred. No trace of them will ever be found.

But in the day of their trouble, there will be rest on the earth. And they will fall down in his presence and not get up. There will be no one to lift them back up, as they have denied the Lord of spirits and his anointed. May the name of the Lord of spirits be blessed!

## 49:1-4.

Wisdom is poured out like water, and magnificence does not fail in his presence for evermore, for all his just secrets are powerful. But wickedness disappears like a shadow, and does not continue, for the chosen one stands in the presence of the Lord of spirits, and his splendor lasts for ever and ever, and his power lasts for all generations.

The spirit of wisdom lives in him, as does the spirit which gives understanding and power, and the spirit of those who have fallen asleep justly. He will judge secret things. No one will be able to tell a lie in his presence, for the chosen one is in the presence of the Lord of Spirits, in accordance with his wish.

## 50:1-5.

In those days the sacred and the chosen ones will change. The light of days will rest on them, and the splendor and glory of the sacred will be changed. In the day of trouble disaster will be heaped up on wrongdoers, but the honest will triumph in the name of the Lord of spirits.

He will show this to others so that they will change their minds and stop what they are doing. They will have no honor in the presence of the Lord of spirits, but by his name they may be rescued. The Lord of spirits will have compassion on them, as he has much compassion. His judgment is just, and wickedness will not be able to stand against his judgment. The one who does not change their mind will perish. "From then on I will not have compassion on them," says the Lord of spirits.

## 51:1-5.

In those days the earth will give back that which has been entrusted to it, and Sheol will return that which has been entrusted to it, that which it has received. Destruction will return what it owes. He will select the honest and sacred from among them, for the day when they will be rescued has approached.

In those days the chosen one will sit on his throne, and all the secrets of wisdom will pour from his mouth, for the Lord of spirits has given them to him and exalted him.

In those days the mountains will skip like rams, and the hills will leap like lambs full of milk, and the faces of all the angels in heaven will be lit up with happiness, for in those days the chosen one will be praised. The earth will celebrate. The honest will live on it, and the chosen ones will walk on it.

## 52:1-9.

After those days in the place where I had seen all the visions of that which is hidden, I was carried away by a whirlwind, and it took me off to the west. There my eyes saw the secrets of heaven, and everything which existed on earth, a mountain of iron, a mountain of copper, a mountain of silver, a mountain of gold, a mountain of soft metal, and a mountain of lead.

I asked the angel who went with me, "What are these things which I have seen in secret?"

He answered me, "All these things which you have seen will be for the anointed one's dominion, so that he may be strong and powerful on the earth."

The angel of peace answered me, "Wait just a short time, and you will see that every secret thing which the Lord of spirits has decreed will be revealed to you. Those mountains which you have seen, the mountain of iron, the mountain of copper, the mountain of silver, the mountain of gold, the mountain of soft metal, and the mountain of lead, all these will melt like wax in a fire in the presence of the chosen one. Like the water that descends from above on these mountains, they will become powerless before his feet. It will come to pass in those days, that people will not be able to save themselves by silver or gold, nor will they be able to flee.

"There will be no iron for war, no material for a breastplate.

Bronze will be of no use, tin will be of no use and will count for nothing, and lead will not be wanted. All these things will be rejected, and destroyed off the face of the earth, when the chosen one appears in the presence of the Lord of spirits."

### 53:1-7.

There my eyes saw a deep valley, and its entrance was open.

Everyone who lives on the earth, on the sea, and on islands, will bring him gifts, presents, and offerings, yet that deep valley will not become full. Their hands will commit wrongdoing. Whatever they produce by working, the wrongdoers will devour with crime. But they will be destroyed in front of the Lord of spirits, and from the face of his earth, incessantly, for ever and ever. I saw the angels of punishment, who were living there, and preparing every instrument of the adversary.

Then I asked the angel of peace, who went with me, "For whom are they preparing these instruments?"

He said, "They are preparing them for the kings and powerful ones of the earth, so that they will perish. After this the honest and chosen one will cause the house of his worshippers to appear, and from then on they will not be hindered anymore, by the name of the Lord of spirits. In his presence these mountains will not be solid like the earth, and the hills will be like fountains of water. And the honest will have rest from oppression by wrongdoers."

### 54:1-10.

Then I looked and turned to another part of the earth, where I saw a deep valley burning with fire. They brought monarchs and the powerful and threw them in this valley. There my eyes saw how they made instruments for them, iron chains of immeasurable weight. Then I asked the angel of peace, who went with me, "For whom are these chain instruments being prepared?"

He replied, "These are being prepared for the hosts of Azazel, so that they may take them and throw them into the lowest part of the abyss, and cover their jaws with rough stones, as the Lord of spirits commanded. Michael, Gabriel, Raphael, and Phanuel will take hold of them on that great day and will throw them into a furnace of blazing fire, so that the Lord of spirits may take vengeance on them for their crimes, because they became servants of the adversary, and led astray those who live on earth.

"In those days the punishment of the Lord of spirits will go out, and the containers of water which are above the heavens, and the fountains which are under the earth, will be opened. All the waters will be mixed with the waters that are above the skies. The water which is above heaven will be the male, and the water which is under the earth will be the female. All the inhabitants of earth will be wiped out and all who live under the ends of heaven will be wiped out. Because of this they will understand the wickedness they have done on earth, and they will be destroyed by these means."

## 55:1-4.

Afterwards the Ancient of Days changed his mind, and said, "I have destroyed all the inhabitants of the earth for no purpose!"

And he swore by his great name, "From now on I will not act like this to all the inhabitants of the earth. But I will place a sign in the heavens, and it will be a guarantee of good faith between me and them forever, as long as the days of heaven and earth last on the earth. This will be in agreement with my command. When I wish to seize them, by the hands of angels, in the day of trouble and pain, I will certainly cause my anger and my rebuke to stay on them," says the Lord, the Lord of spirits. "You powerful kings who live on the earth, you will see my chosen one sitting on my splendid throne. And he will judge Azazel, all his associates, and all his hosts, in the name of the Lord of spirits."

## 56:1-8.

There I saw hosts of the angels of punishment, as they went, and they were holding chains of iron and bronze. Then I asked the angel of peace, who went with me, "To whom are those angels who are holding the chains going?"

He answered, "To their chosen and loved ones, so that they may be thrown into the chasm of the valley's abyss, and then that valley will be filled with their chosen and their loved ones, and the days of their life will be at an end, but the days of their leading astray will be innumerable.

"In those days, the angels will assemble, and will throw themselves towards the east, on the Parthians and Medes. They will stir kings, so that a spirit of unrest comes on them. They will fling them from their thrones, and will spring out like lions from their dens, like hungry wolves in the middle of the flock. They will go up and trample underfoot the land of his chosen ones, and the land of my chosen ones will become a threshing floor and beaten path in front of them. The land of their chosen ones will be in front of them. But the city of my just ones will hinder their horses. They will begin to fight amongst themselves, and their own right hand will be strong against them. A person will not acknowledge their friend or sibling, or a child their father or mother, until the number of the corpses is fulfilled, and their punishment will be not in vain. In those days Sheol will open its mouth, and they will be swallowed up in it and destroyed. Sheol will swallow up wrongdoers in the presence of the chosen."

## 57:1-3.

After this I saw another army of chariots with men riding in them. They came on winds from the east, from the west, and from the south. The sound of the noise of their chariots was heard and when that uproar happened, the sacred ones observed it from heaven and the pillars of the earth shook from their foundations. The sound of it was heard from the ends of the earth and to the ends of heaven at the same time. And they will all fall down, and worship the Lord of spirits. This is the end of the second parable.

## The Third Parable

## 58:1-6.

I now began to speak the third parable, about the honest and the chosen. Blessed are you, you honest and chosen, for your allotment will be magnificent! The honest will be in the light of the sun, and the chosen in the light of eternal life, the days of their life will never end, and the days of the sacred will be without number. They will seek the light and will find justice with the Lord of spirits.

There will be peace for the honest with the Lord of the world. After this the sacred will be told to seek in heaven the secrets of justice and the share of faith, for it has become as bright as the sun on the earth, while darkness has passed away. There will be light which never ends, and they will not come to the limit of time, for darkness will first have been destroyed, and light will last in the presence of the Lord of spirits. The light of justice will last in the presence of the Lord of spirits forever.


## 59:1-3.

In those days my eyes saw the secrets of the lightnings and the lights, and their judgment. They lighten for a blessing or for a curse, according to the desire of the Lord of spirits. There I saw the secrets of the thunder, when it booms above in heaven, how its sound is heard. The judgments of the earth were shown to me, whether for peace and for a blessing, or for a curse, according to the word of the Lord of spirits. Afterwards all the secrets of the lights and of the lightnings were shown to me, and they cause light for blessing and for satisfaction.


## The Book of Noah - a fragment


## 60:1-24.

In the five hundredth year, and in the seventh month, on the fourteenth day of the month, in the life of Enoch. In that vision, I saw that the heaven of heavens was shaken fiercely, and that the host of the Most High, and the angels, thousands and thousands, and ten thousand times ten thousand, were agitated and greatly disturbed. And when I looked, the Ancient of Days was sitting on his splendid throne, while the angels and the honest were standing around him. A great trembling seized me, and terror took hold of me. My loins buckled and gave way, my strength dissolved, and I fell on my face.

Then sacred Michael sent another sacred angel, one of the sacred ones, and he raised me up, and when he raised me, my spirit returned, for I had been unable to endure the sight of the host, the disturbance, and the shaking of heaven.

Then sacred Michael said to me, "Why are you disturbed by this vision? The time of compassion lasted until now, and he has been compassionate and patient towards all the inhabitants of the earth. But the day will come when the power, the punishment, and the judgment will take place, which the Lord of spirits has prepared for those who do not worship the just judgment, those who deny that judgment, and for those who take his name in vain. That day has been prepared for the chosen as a day of covenant, and for wrongdoers as a day of inquisition."

On that day two monsters will be separated from one another, a female monster named Leviathan, (43) to live in the depths of the sea, above the springs of waters, and a male monster named Behemoth, which moves on its chest, and occupies a large desert named Dendayen in the east of the garden, where the chosen and the just live, where my grandfather was received. My grandfather was human, the seventh from Adam, the first human whom the Lord of spirits made. Then I asked the other angel to show me the power of those monsters, how they became separated on the same day, one being thrown into the depths of the sea, and one onto the dry desert. He answered, "You, human, are here wishing to understand secret things."

And the angel of peace, who was with me, said, "These two monsters are prepared by God's power so that God's punishment won't be in vain. Then children will be slain with their mothers, and sons with their fathers. When the punishment of the Lord of spirits comes on them, it will continue, so that the punishment of the Lord of spirits won't take place in vain. After that, judgment will be with compassion and patience."

Then another angel, who went with me, spoke to me, and showed me the first and last secrets in heaven above, and in the depths of the earth, in the ends of heaven, and its foundations, and in the container of the winds. He showed me how the winds were divided, how they were balanced, and how both the springs and the winds were numbered according to their power. He showed me the power of the moon's light, that its power is a fitting one, as well as the divisions of the stars, according to their respective names, how every division is divided.

He showed me that the lightning flashes, that its host immediately obeys, and that it stops during the progression of the sound of thunder. Thunder and lightning are not separated. They do not occur together, yet they are not separate. For when the lightning flashes, the thunder sounds, and their essence pauses at a proper interval, making an equal division between them, as the container, on which their intervals depend, is as flexible as sand. Each of them at their proper time is bridled and turned by the power of their essence, which propels them as far as the whole extent of the earth.

The essence of the sea is also powerful and strong, and a strong power causes it to ebb, and drives it forwards, and it disperses amongst the mountains of the earth. The essence of the frost has its angel, in the essence of hail there is a good angel, the essence of snow leaves its own place due to its strength, and a special essence is in it, which ascends from it like vapor, and is called frost. The essence of mist does not live with them in their container, but it has a container to itself, for its progress is majestic in light, and in darkness, in winter and in summer. Its container is bright, and an angel is in it.

The spirit of dew lives in the extremities of heaven, and is connected with the containers of rain, and its progress is in winter and in summer. The cloud produced by it, and the cloud of the mist, are connected. One gives to the other, and when the spirit of rain is in motion from its container, angels come and open its container and bring it out. When it too is sprinkled over all the earth, it forms a union with every kind of water on the ground. The waters stay on the ground, because they give nourishment to the earth from the Most High, who is in heaven. For this reason there is a regulation in the quantity of rain, and the angels are in charge of it.

.I saw all these things near the garden of justice.

**61:1-13**.

In those days I saw long cords given to those angels, who took to their wings, and flew, advancing towards the north. I asked the angel, "Where have they taken those long cords, and gone off?"

He said, "They have gone off to measure."

The angel, who went with me, said, "These are the measures of the just, and the just bring cords, so that they may depend on the name of the Lord of spirits for ever and ever. The chosen will begin to live with the chosen. And these are the measures which will be given to faith, and which will strengthen justice. These measures will reveal all the secrets of the depths of the earth and those who have been destroyed in the desert, and those who have been devoured by the fish of the sea, and by wild beasts, will return, and rely on the day of the chosen one, for none will perish in the presence of the Lord of spirits, nor will any be capable of perishing.

"And all who live in the heavens above received a command, a power, one voice, and one light like fire. And they blessed him with their voice, they exalted him, and they praised him with wisdom. They were wise with their speech, and with the breath of life. Then the Lord of spirits seated the chosen one on his splendid throne. He will judge all the deeds of the sacred, in heaven above, and will weigh their actions in a balance. When he lifts up his face to judge their secret ways in accordance with the word of the name of the Lord of spirits, and their progress along the path in accordance with the just judgment of the Lord most high, then they will all speak with united voice, and bless, praise, exalt, and extol, the name of the Lord of spirits. "He will call all the host of the heavens, and all the sacred ones above, and the host of God, the Cherubim, the Seraphim, and the Ophanin, all the powerful angels, and all the angels of the principalities, and the chosen one, and the other host that is on earth and over the water on that day.

"They will raise their united voice, and will bless, praise, and exalt with the spirit of faith, with the spirit of wisdom and patience, with the spirit of compassion, with the spirit of judgment and peace, and with the spirit of goodwill. All will say with united voice, 'Blessed is he, and may the name of the Lord of spirits be blessed for ever and ever.'

"All who do not sleep in heaven above will bless him. All the sacred ones in heaven will bless him, all the chosen who live in the garden of life, and every spirit of light, who is capable of blessing, praising, exalting, and extolling your sacred name, and all of the natural realm will beyond measure praise and bless your name for ever and ever. For the compassion of the Lord of spirits is vast. He is patient. All his works and all his power, all the great things he has done, he has revealed to the just and to the chosen, in the name of the Lord of spirits."

## 62:1-16.

Thus the Lord commanded the kings, the mighty, the exalted, and the inhabitants of the earth, "Open your eyes, and raise your horns, if you are able to recognize the chosen one."

The Lord of spirits seated him on his splendid throne. The spirit of justice was poured out over him. The word of his mouth will destroy all the wrongdoers and all the unjust, who will perish in his presence. In that day all the kings, the mighty, the exalted, and those who possess the earth, will stand up, see, and perceive that he is sitting on his splendid throne, and that the just are judged justly in his presence, and no useless word is spoken in his presence.

Then pain will come on them, as on a woman in childbirth whose labor is severe, when her child comes to the mouth of the womb, and she has difficulty birthing. One part of them will look at the other. They will be astounded, and have downcast faces. Pain will seize them, when they see this human sitting on his splendid throne.

Then the kings, the mighty, and all who possess the earth, will praise him who has dominion over all things, him who was hidden, for from the beginning the human existed in secret, and the Most High kept him in the presence of his power, and revealed him to the chosen. The assembly of the sacred and of the chosen will be sown, and all the chosen will stand in his presence on that day. All the kings, the mighty, the exalted, and those who rule over all the earth, will fall down on their faces in worship before him. They will set their hope on this human, will pray to him, and petition him to show compassion.

Then the Lord of spirits will hurry to expel them from his presence. Their faces will be full of confusion, and darkness will grow deeper on their faces. The angels of punishment will take them, so that they will be repaid for the wrong done to his children and his chosen.

They will become an exhibition to the just and to his chosen. They will celebrate because of them, as the anger of the Lord of spirits will rest on them. Then the sword of the Lord of spirits will be drunk with their blood, but the just and the chosen will be safe on that day, and they will never again see the face of the wrongdoers and the unjust.

The Lord of spirits will remain over them, and they will live, eat, lie down, and get up, with this human, for ever and ever. The just and the chosen have risen from the earth, have stopped having downcast faces, have stopped having depressed appearances, and have put on the clothing of life. The clothing of life is from the Lord of spirits, in whose presence your clothing will not get old, nor will your magnificence decrease.

### 63:1-12.

In those days the mighty kings who possess the earth will beg the angels of his punishment, to whom they have been handed over, to give them a little rest, so that they may fall down and worship in the presence of the Lord of spirits, and admit their wrongdoings to him. And they will bless and praise the Lord of spirits: "Blessed is the Lord of spirits, the Lord of kings, the Lord of the mighty, the Lord of the rich, the Lord of splendor, and the Lord of wisdom. Every secret thing is clear to you, and your power lasts for generation after generation, and your splendor lasts for ever and ever. Your secrets are deep and numberless, and your justice is beyond measure. Now we realize that we should praise and bless the Lord of kings and him who is king over all kings." They will say, "If only we could have some rest so we could praise, thank, and bless him, and admit our wrongdoings in the presence of his splendor?"

And now we long for a little rest but do not find it, we are driven away and do not possess it. Light has passed away from in front of us, and darkness will be where we will live for ever. For we have not believed him, we have not praised the name of the Lord of spirits, we have not praised the Lord for all his works, but we have trusted the scepter of our kingdom and of our magnificence.

On the day of our affliction and of our trouble he will not save us, neither will we find any rest to agree that our Lord is faithful in all his actions, in all his judgments, and in his justice. His judgments have no respect for persons, and we must leave his presence on account of our deeds as our wrongdoings are certainly without number. Then will they say to themselves, "Our inner beings are full of criminal gain, but that doesn't prevent us from going down into the fiery middle of Sheol!"

Afterwards, their faces will be filled with darkness and confusion before the human, and they will be driven from his presence, and the sword will remain in their midst, in his presence. The Lord of spirits says, "This is the decree and the judgment against the mighty, the kings, the exalted, and those who possess the earth, in the presence of the Lord of spirits."

## 64:1-2. (44)

I also saw other figures hidden in that place. I heard the voice of an angel saying, "These are the angels who went down from heaven to earth, and have revealed what is hidden to the humans, and seduced the humans into doing wrong."

## 65:1-12. (45)

In those days Noah saw that the earth had tilted, and that destruction approached. He set off from there and went to the ends of the earth, and called out to his grandfather Enoch. Noah said three times with a bitter voice, "Hear me, hear me, hear me!"

And I said to him, "Tell me, what is happening to the earth, as it is so badly affected and violently shaken, surely I will perish with it!"

Then immediately there was a great disturbance on the earth, and a voice was heard from heaven. I fell down on my face. Then my grandfather Enoch came and stood by me, and said, "Why have you cried out to me so bitterly and wept? A decree has gone out from the Lord against the inhabitants of the earth, that they must be destroyed. They know all the secrets of the angels, and all the oppressive and secret powers of the satans, and every power of those who commit sorcery, and the power of those who make molten images in the whole earth. They know how silver is produced from the dust of the earth, and how soft metal originates from the earth. For lead and tin are not produced from earth like the former, for there is a spring that produces them, and there is an angel standing on it, and that angel allocates them."

Afterwards my grandfather Enoch seized me with his hand, and raised me up, and said to me, "Go! I have asked the Lord of spirits about this disturbance on the earth, and he replied, 'Because of their wickedness, their judgment has been completed, and I will not withhold it, forever. Because of the sorceries which they have searched out and learnt, the earth and its inhabitants shall be destroyed. There will be no place of refuge for them forever because they showed them what was hidden, and they are damned. But this is not the case with you, my son. The Lord of spirits knows that you are good, and innocent of the reproach concerning the secrets. He has established your name in the midst of the sacred ones, and will preserve you from amongst the inhabitants of the earth. He has destined your just offspring for dominion and great honor, and countless numbers of the just and the sacred will flow from your offspring forever."

## 66:1-3. (46)

After this he showed me the angels of punishment, who were ready to come and release all the force of the waters under the earth in order to bring judgment and destruction of all the inhabitants of the earth. The Lord of spirits commanded the angels who were going out not to make the waters rise but to keep an eye on them, for those angels were in charge of the force of the waters. Then I left Enoch.

## 67:1-13. (47)

In those days God's word came to me, and said, "Noah, your allotment has come up before me, an allotment void of blame, an allotment of love and justice. Now the angels are working with a timber, but when they have finished this, I will place my hand on it, and preserve it. The seed of life will come out of it, and a change will take place, so that the earth will not be left empty. I will establish your offspring before me for ever and ever, and I will scatter those who live with you over the face of the earth. It will not happen again on the earth. They will be blessed and multiplied on the earth, in the name of the Lord."

67

They will lock up those angels who acted wickedly in that burning valley, which my grandfather Enoch had previously shown me in the west, where there were mountains of gold and silver, of iron, of soft metal, and of tin. I saw that valley in which there was a great disturbance, and where the waters heaved.

And when all this happened, a smell of sulfur was produced from the fiery molten metal and the disturbance which troubled them in that place, and the smell came from the waters. The valley of the angels who had been guilty of leading humans astray, burned underneath the ground. Rivers of fire flowed through that valley, where those angels who led the inhabitants of the earth astray will be condemned.

But in those days, those waters will be for healing the inner self and the body, and for judgment of the spirit, for kings, the mighty, the exalted, and the inhabitants of the earth. Their spirits will be full of lust and they will be judged in their bodies, because they have denied the Lord of spirits, and although they see their punishment daily, they do not believe his name.

The more they are burned, the more a change will take place in their spirits for ever and ever, for no one can speak a useless word in the presence of the Lord of spirits. Judgment will come on them, because they trusted their bodily lust, but denied the spirit of the Lord. In those days the waters of that valley will be changed, for when the angels are judged, the temperature of those springs of water will change. When the angels come up, the water of the springs will change, and become cold. Then I heard the sacred Michael answering. He said, "This judgment by which the angels are judged, will bear witness against the kings and the mighty who possess the earth. For these waters of judgment will be for their healing, and for the lust of their bodies. But they will not recognize and believe that the waters will change and become a fire which burns forever."

**68:1-5**.

After this my grandfather Enoch gave me the signs of all the secrets in the book, and of the parables which had been given to him, and he inserted them for me in the words of the book of parables. At that that time the sacred Michael answered and said to Raphael, "Spiritual power seizes me, and urges me on because of the severity of the angels' judgment. Who can endure the severe judgment which has been executed, before which they melt away?"

Again the sacred Michael answered the sacred Raphael, "Who is there whose heart is not softened by it, and whose mind is not disturbed by this word? Judgment has gone out against them by those who have dragged them away!"

But it came to pass that when they stood in the presence of the Lord of spirits, the sacred Michael said to Raphael, "I will not take their part under the Lord's eye, because the Lord of spirits has been angry with them because they acted as if they were masters.

Because of this the secret judgment will come on them for ever and ever, and neither angel nor human will receive any part of it, but they alone will receive their judgment for ever end ever.

## 69:1-29.

"After this judgment they will be terrified and shaken, because they have shown this to the inhabitants of the earth."

Here are the names of those angels! The first of them is Semjaza, the second, Artiqifa, the third, Armen, the fourth, Kokabel, the fifth, Turael, the sixth, Rumjal, the seventh, Danjal, the eighth, Nuqael, the ninth, Baraqel, the tenth, Azazel, the eleventh, Armaros, the twelfth, Batarjal, the thirteenth, Busasajel, the fourteenth, Hananel, the fifteenth, Turel, the sixteenth, Simapesiel, the seventeenth, Yetarel, the eighteenth, Tumael, the nineteenth, Turel, the twentieth, Rumael, the twenty-first, Azazel. These are the chiefs of their angels, and the names of the leaders of their hundreds, and the leaders of their fifties, and the leaders of their tens.

The name of the first is Jeqon. He was the one who led all the sacred associates of God astray and brought them down to earth, and led them astray with humans. The name of the second is Asbeel. He suggested an evil plan to the sacred associates of God, so that they defiled their bodies with humans. The name of the third is Gadreel. He showed every deadly blow to the humans. He led Eve astray, and showed the humans the weapons of death, the coat of mail, the shield, and the sword for killing, every deadly weapon he showed to the humans. Because of him they have proceeded against the inhabitants of the earth for ever and ever.

The name of the fourth is Penemue. He showed humans bitterness and sweetness, and showed them all the secrets of their wisdom. He taught humans writing with ink and paper, and through that, numerous have gone astray through every time of the world, even to this day. For humans were not born for this, to confirm their faith with pen and ink. For humans were created just like the angels, so that they would stay just and pure, and death, which destroys everything, would not have touched them. But they perish because of this knowledge, and death consumes them through this power.

The name of the fifth is Kasdeja. He showed the humans every wicked strike of spirits and of demons, the strike at the embryo in the womb, to miscarry it, the strike of the spirit by the bite of the serpent, and the strike which is given in the midday by the offspring of the serpent, the name of which is Tabaaet.

This is the task of Kasbeel, the chief of the oath which he showed to the sacred ones when he lived in splendor. His name is Biqa. He told sacred Michael to show him the secret name, so that they might say it in the oath, so that those who showed every secret thing to the humans would shake at that name and oath. This is the power of that oath, for it is powerful and strong. He placed this oath Akae in the charge of the sacred Michael.

These are the secrets of this oath, and they are strong through this oath. Heaven was suspended by it before the world was created, and forever. By it the earth was founded on the water, and from the secret parts of the mountains the beautiful waters come, from the creation of the world to eternity. By that oath the sea was created, and its foundation. During the time of anger he placed the sand against it, and this continues unchanged forever. By this oath the depths were made firm, and they do not move from their place, for ever and ever.

By that oath the sun and moon complete their course, never wandering from the regulation given to them for ever and ever. By this oath the stars complete their course, and he calls their names, and they answer him, for ever and ever.

In same goes for the spirits of the water, and of the winds, and of all the breezes, and their paths from all the groups of spirits. There the containers of thunder's voices are kept, and the light of the lightning. There the containers of hail and of frost, and the containers of snow, the containers of rain and of dew are kept. All these believe and praise in the presence of the Lord of spirits and praise him with all their power. He sustains them with every act of thanks, while they praise, extol, and exalt the name of the Lord of spirits for ever and ever.

This oath is strong over them. Through it, they are kept safe and their progress is preserved. They were very happy, and they blessed, praised, and exalted, because the name of the human was revealed to them. He sat on his splendid throne, and the whole judgment was assigned to him, the human. Wrongdoers will disappear and perish from the face of the earth, while those who led them astray will be bound with chains for ever. They will be imprisoned in the assembly place of their destruction, and all their works will disappear from the face of the earth. From then on there will be nothing to corrupt, for the human has appeared, sitting on his splendid throne. Everything wicked will disappear and leave his presence, and the human's word will be powerful in the presence of the Lord of spirits. This is the third parable of Enoch.

## The Storehouses
### 70:1-4.

It came to pass, that after this, during his lifetime, his name was lifted up by the inhabitants of the earth to the presence of the human, and to the presence of the Lord of spirits. He was lifted by the spiritual chariots, and his name vanished among them. From that time I was no longer counted among them, but he sat me between two winds, between the north and the west, where the angels took the ropes to measure for me the place for the chosen and the just. There I saw the ancestors of the first humans, and the sacred, who live in that place for ever.

### 71:1-17.

And it came to pass after this that my spirit was carried away, and went up into the heavens. I saw the sacred associates of God treading on flaming fire. Their garments and clothes were white, and their faces were as light as snow. I saw two rivers of fire glittering like a hyacinth. Then I fell on my face in the presence of the Lord of spirits. The angel Michael, one of the archangels, took me by my right hand, lifted me up, and led me to where there were all the secrets of compassion and secrets of justice. He showed me all the secrets of the extremities of heaven, all the containers of the stars, and the luminaries, from where they come out in the presence of the sacred ones.

And he carried off Enoch to the heaven of heavens. There I saw, in the middle of that light, a structure made with ice crystals, and in the middle of these crystals were tongues of living fire. My spirit saw a circle of fire, and it surrounded the fiery structure. All around it were rivers full of living fire. The Seraphim, the Cherubim, and Ophanin surrounded it. These are those who never sleep, but guard his splendid throne. And I saw innumerable angels, thousands of thousands, and ten thousand times ten thousand, surrounding that structure. Michael, Raphael, Gabriel, Phanuel and the sacred angels who were in the heavens above, went in and out of it. Michael, Raphael, Gabriel, and innumerable sacred angels went out of that structure.

With them was the Ancient of Days. His face was white and pure as wool, and his clothing was indescribable. Then I fell on my face, my whole body melted, and my spirit became changed. I cried out loudly, with a powerful spirit, blessing, praising, and exalting. And those blessings which came out of my mouth were pleasing in the presence of the Ancient of Days. The Ancient of Days came with Michael, Gabriel, Raphael, and Phanuel, and with thousands of thousands, and thousands and ten thousands of angels without number.

Then that angel came to me, and greeted me with his voice, "You are a human who was born for justice, and justice has rested on you and the justice of the Ancient of Days will not leave you." He continued, "He proclaims peace to you in the name of the world which is to come, for from there peace has gone out since the world was created. And so it will be for you for ever and ever. All who will exist, and who will walk in your pathway of justice, will never leave you. They will live with you. You will be their allotment, and they will not be separated from you for ever and ever. So long life will be with that human, and the just will have peace, and the just will walk along the pathway of integrity, in the name of the Lord of spirits, for ever and ever.

72

## The book of the revolutions of the heavenly luminaries 72:1-37.

The book of the revolutions of the heavenly luminaries, according to their respective classes, their respective powers and seasons, their respective names and places of origin, and their respective months, which Uriel, the sacred angel who was with me and is their guide, showed me. He showed me all their regulations, for each year of the world and forever, until a new creation is made, which will be eternal.

This is the first law of the luminaries. The luminary, the sun, rises in the portals of heaven, which are on the east, and sets in the west in the western portals of heaven. I saw six portals from where the sun rises, and six portals where the sun sets. The moon rises and sets in these portals. I saw the leaders of the stars, together with those whom they lead. There are six in the east and six in the west. All these, one after the other, are in the same place, and there are numerous windows on the right and on the left sides of those portals.

First that great luminary called the sun goes out. Its orb is like the heaven's orb, the whole of it being filled with splendid and flaming fire. The wind blows the chariot on which it ascends. The sun sets in heaven, and, returning by the north, goes to the east, and is led so as to enter by that portal, and illuminate the face of the sky. In the same manner it goes out by the large portal in the first month. It goes out through the fourth of those six portals, which are in the east. And in the fourth portal, through which the sun rises in the first month, are twelve window-openings, and a flame goes out of them whenever they are opened at their proper time.

When the sun rises in heaven, it goes out through this fourth portal for thirty days, and sets exactly in the fourth portal in the west of heaven. During that time the day grows longer daily, and the night grows shorter nightly until the thirtieth morning. On that day the day is longer by two parts than the night. The day amounts to precisely ten parts, and the night to eight parts. The sun rises through this fourth portal, and sets in it, and returns to the fifth portal in the east for thirty days, and rises from it, and sets in the fifth portal.

Then the day becomes longer by two parts, so the day amounts to eleven parts, while the night becomes shorter, amounting to seven parts. The sun now returns to the east, entering the sixth portal, and rising and setting in the sixth portal for thirty-one mornings, on account of its sign. On that day, the day is longer than the night, being twice as long as the night, and the day becomes twelve parts, and the night becomes shorter and amounts to six parts. Then the sun rises so that the day may be shortened, and the night lengthened. And the sun returns to the east and enters the sixth portal, where it rises and sets for thirty days.

When that has happened, the day becomes shortened by precisely one part, so that it is eleven parts, while the night is seven parts. Then the sun goes from that sixth portal in the west, and goes to the east, rising in the fifth portal for thirty days, and setting again in the fifth portal of the west. At that time the day becomes shortened by two parts, so that is ten parts, while the night is eight parts. Then the sun goes out from the fifth portal, and sets in the fifth portal of the west, and rises in the fourth portal for thirty-one days, on account of its signs, and sets in the west. At that time the day is made equal with the night and, being equal with it, the night amounts to nine parts, and the day to nine parts.

Then the sun goes out from that portal, and sets in the west, and returns to the east by the third portal for thirty days, and sets in the west at the third portal. At that time the night decreases in length, and the night amounts to ten parts and the day to eight. The sun then rises from the third portal, as it sets in the west and returns to the east. It rises in the third portal of the east for thirty one days and sets in the west.

In the same way too it sets in the second portal in the west of heaven. At that time the night is eleven parts, and the day is seven parts. Then at that time the sun goes from the second portal, as it sets in the second portal in the west, but returns to the east by the first portal for thirty-one days, and sets in the west in the first portal.

At that time that night is lengthened as much as the day. It is precisely twelve parts, while the day is six parts. The sun has thus completed its beginnings, and a second time goes around from these beginnings. In that first portal it enters for thirty days, and sets in the opposite part of heaven in the west. At that time the length of the night is shortened by a fourth part, that is, one portion, and becomes eleven parts. The day is seven parts.

74

Then the sun returns, and enters the second portal in the east. It returns on these divisions for thirty days, rising and setting. At that time the night decreases in length. It becomes ten parts, and the day eight parts. Then the sun goes from that second portal, and sets in the west, but returns to the east, and rises in the third portal in the east for thirty-one days, setting in the west of the sky. At that time the night becomes shortened. It is nine parts. The night is equal to the day. The year is precisely three hundred and sixty-four days. The length of the day and night and the shortness of the day and night, are different from each other by the progress of the sun. By means of this progress the day is lengthened daily, and the night is greatly shortened. This is the sun's regulation and progress, and its return, returning for sixty days, and going out. This is the great everlasting luminary, that which is named the sun, for ever and ever.

That is a great luminary which goes forth, and which is named after its kind, as the Lord commanded. And thus it rises and sets, neither getting shorter nor resting, but running on by day and by night. It shines a seventh portion of light more than the moon, but the dimensions of both are equal.


## 73:1-8.

After this law I saw another law of a lesser luminary, named the moon, the shape of which is like the shape of the sun. The wind blows the chariot on which it rides, and light is given to it by the measure. Every month its rising and setting change and its days are like the days of the sun. When its light is full, its light is a seventh part of the sun's light.

And it rises like this, and its first phase is to the east: it rises on the thirtieth day. At that time it appears and becomes the first phase of the moon for you on the thirtieth day, together with the sun in the portal from which the sun goes out. One half of it goes out by a seventh part, and the whole of its orb is empty of light, except for a seventh part, the fourteenth part of its light. And in a day it receives a seventh part, or half that part, of its light. Its light is one seventh and a half. It sets with the sun, and when the sun rises, the moon rises with it, receiving half a part of light. On that night, at the beginning of its morning, at the beginning of the moon's day, the moon sets with the sun and on that night it is dark in its fourteen and half parts. But it rises on that day with precisely one seventh part, and it goes out and recedes from the rising of the sun. During the remainder of its time its light increases. (48)

## 74:1-17.

Then I saw another course and regulation and how it makes its monthly journey according to that regulation. Uriel, the sacred angel who is the leader of them all, showed me all these and their positions, and I wrote down their positions as he showed them to me. I wrote down their months as they occur, and the appearance of their lights, until fifteen days have passed.

It completes its setting in the west in seven parts and completes its rising in the east in seven parts. But in certain months it changes its settings, and in certain months it makes its own way. In two months the moon sets with the sun, that is, in those two portals which are in the middle, in the third and fourth portal. It goes out for seven days, then returns to the portal from where the sun goes out, and in that completes its whole light. Then it recedes from the sun, and in eight days enters the sixth portal from which the sun rises. When the sun rises from the fourth portal, the moon goes out for seven days, until it rises from the fifth portal. Then it returns in seven days to the fourth portal, and completing all its light, recedes, and enters the first portal in eight days.

Thus I saw their position, according to the fixed order of the months the sun rises and sets At those times there is a surplus of thirty days of the sun in five years, and all the days add up to each year of the five years, and amount to 364 days. The surplus of the sun and stars amounts to 6 days, 6 days in each of the 5 years, thus 30 days. Thus the moon has 30 days less than the sun and stars.

The moon carries out all the years precisely, so that their positions may come neither too early nor too late even for a single day, but change the year in precisely in 364 days. In 3 years the days are 1092 days, in 5 years 1820 days, and in 8 years there are 2912 days.

For the moon alone, the days in 3 years amount to 1,062 days, and in 5 years amount to 50 days behind. In 5 years there are 1,770 days so that the days of the moon in eight years amount to 2,832 days. In 8 years the difference is 80 days, by which it falls short. The year then becomes completed according to the position of the moon and

76

the position of the sun, as they rise from the portal in which the sun rises and sets for 30 days.

**75:1-9.**

These are the leaders of the chiefs of the thousands, those which preside over the whole creation and over all the stars, with the four days which are added and never separated from their allotted place, according to the calculation of the year. And these serve the four days which are not calculated in the calculation of the year. People go greatly wrong because of these, as these luminaries truly serve in the stations of the world, one in the first portal, one in the third portal, one in the fourth portal, and one in the sixth portal. And the harmony of the world is completed by the 364 stations.

The signs, the seasons, the years, and the days, were shown to me by Uriel, the angel whom the splendid Lord appointed over all the heavenly luminaries of the sky and the world, so that they would rule in the face of the sky, and appear over the earth, and become leaders of the days and nights: the sun, the moon, the stars, and all the serving creatures which make their circuit with all the heavenly chariots

Likewise, Uriel showed me twelve portals open for the circle of the chariots of the sun in the sky, from which the rays of the sun shoot forth. From them heat comes out over the earth, when they are opened in their appointed seasons. They are for the winds, and the spirit of the dew, when in their seasons they are opened, being opened in the extremities of the heavens. I saw twelve portals in heaven at the extremities of the earth, through which the sun, moon, and stars, and all the works of heaven, rise and set. Many windows also are open on the right and on the left. One window at its appointed season grows hot corresponding to those portals from which the stars go out as they are commanded, and in which they set corresponding to their number. I also saw the heavenly chariots, running in the world, above those portals in which the stars turn, which never set. One of these is bigger than all the others, and it goes around the whole world.

**76:1-14.**

And at the extremities of the earth I saw twelve portals open for all the winds, from which they go out and blow over the earth. Three of them are open in the front of heaven, three in the back, three on the right side of heaven, and three on the left. The first three are those which are towards the east, three are towards the north, three behind those which are on the left, to the south, and three on the west. From four of them winds of blessing and of health go out, and from eight of them winds of punishment go out in order to destroy the earth, all its inhabitants, and everything that is in the waters or on dry land.

The first of these winds goes from the portal called the eastern, through the first portal on the east. The one that goes from the south brings destruction, drought, heat, and devastation. From the second portal, the middle one, goes fairness. From it go rain, fruitfulness, prosperity, and dew. From the third portal which is northwards, go cold and drought. After these the south winds come out through three portals. A hot wind comes through the first portal, which is to the east. But from the middle portal come lovely fragrances, dew, rain, prosperity, and life. Dew, rain, locusts, and destruction go out from the third portal, which is to the west.

After these are the north winds. From the seventh portal on the east, come dew, rain, locusts, and destruction. From the portal exactly in the middle come rain, dew, life, and prosperity. From the third portal which is to the west, come mist, frost, snow, rain, dew, and locusts. After these are the west winds. Through the first portal, which is to the north, come dew, rain, frost, cold, snow, and ice. From the middle portal come dew, rain, prosperity, and blessing. Through the last portal, which is to the south, come drought, destruction, scorching, and devastation. The account of the twelve portals of the four quarters of heaven is complete. I have explained to you all their regulations, all their infliction of punishment, and the good produced by them, my son Methuselah.

**77:1-8**.

The first quarter is called the eastern, because it is the first. The second is called the south, because the Most High descends there, he who is blessed forever and descends there frequently. The western quarter is named "reduced", because there all the luminaries of heaven are diminished and go down. The fourth quarter, which is named the "north", is divided into three parts, one of which is for human habitation, another for seas of water, with the deeps, forests, rivers, shady places, and mist, and the third part contains the garden of justice.

I saw seven high mountains, higher than all the mountains of the earth, and snow comes from them, while days, seasons, and years depart and pass away. I saw seven rivers on the earth larger than all rivers, one of which comes from the west and flows into the Great Sea. Two come from the north to the sea, and their waters flow into the Red Sea in the east. And the remaining four flow out on the north side, to their seas, two to the Red Sea, and two into the Great Sea, where it is also said there is a desert. I saw seven large islands, in the sea and on the earth, and five in the Great Sea.


## 78:1-17.

The names of the sun are these: the first Orjares, and the second Tomas. The moon has four names. The first is Asonja, the second, Ebla, the third, Benase, and the fourth, Erae. These are the two great luminaries, whose orbs are like the orbs of heaven, and the dimensions of both appear equal. In the orb of the sun there are seven portions of light, which is added to it more than to the moon and light is transferred to the moon until a seventh portion of the light of the sun is depleted. Then they set and enter the western portal, and make their circuit by the north, and go out over the face of heaven through the eastern portal.

When the moon rises, it, one fourteenth portion of light is all that appears in heaven. In fourteen days the whole of its light is full. But fifteen parts of light are transferred to it until the fifteenth day when its light is full, according to the signs of the year, and it becomes fifteen parts, and the moon grows by the addition of fourteen parts.

During its waning on the first day the moon's light decreases to a fourteenth part, on the second day it decreases to a thirteenth part, on the third day to a twelfth part, on the fourth day to an eleventh part, on the fifth day to a tenth part, on the sixth day to a ninth part, on the seventh day it decreases to an eighth part, on the eighth day it decreases to a seventh part, on the ninth day it decreases to a sixth part, on the tenth day it decreases to a fifth part, on the eleventh day it decreases to a fourth part, on the twelfth day it decreases to a third part, on the thirteenth day it decreases to a second part, on the fourteenth day it decreases to a half of its seventh part, and on the fifteenth day the remainder of its light disappears fully.

On certain months the moon has twenty-nine days and once twenty-eight days. And Uriel showed me another regulation: when light is poured into the moon, and on which side it is poured into it by the sun.

All the time that the moon's light is increasing; it is transferring it to itself when opposite the sun, until in fourteen days its light is full in the sky. And when it is wholly lit up, its light is full in the sky. On the first day it is called the new moon, for on that day light rises on it. It becomes a full moon on the day that the sun sets in the west, while the moon ascends at night from the east. The moon then shines all the night, until the sun rises opposite it, when the moon is seen opposite the sun. On the side on which the moon's light appears, it wanes there again until all its light disappears, and

and the days of the month are at an end. Then its orb remains empty of light.

For three months it achieves thirty days at its proper time, and for three more months it achieves twenty-nine days, during which it effects its waning in the first period of time, and in the first portal for 177 days. And at the time of its rising for three months it appears for thirty days each month, and for three more months it appears twenty-nine days each month. In the night for twenty days each time it looks like a human face, and by day like heaven, and there is nothing else in it except its light.


## 79:1-6.

And now, my son Methuselah, I have shown you everything, and the account of every regulation of the stars of heaven is finished. He showed me every regulation for these, and for every time, and for every rule, and for every year, and for its end, for the order prescribed to it for every month and every week. He showed me also the waning of the moon, which takes place in the sixth portal. Its light becomes full in the sixth portal and after that it is the beginning of the month. Its waning happens in the first portal, at its proper time, until 177 days are completed - according to the mode of calculation by weeks, twenty-five weeks and two days. It falls behind the sun, according to the regulation of the stars; by five days in one period of time when it has completed the pathway you have seen. Such is the appearance and likeness of every luminary, which Uriel, the great angel who is their leader, showed me.

## 80:1-8.

In those days Uriel answered me, "I have showed you everything, Enoch, and I have revealed everything to you. You see the sun, the moon, and the leaders of the stars of heaven, which cause all their operations, seasons, and departures. The years will be shortened in the times of wrongdoers. Their offspring will be backward in their prolific soil, and everything done on earth will be subverted, and will not appear in its season. The rain will be held back, and heaven will withhold it. In those days the fruits of the earth will be late, and will not flourish at their proper time, and in their season the fruits of the trees will be withheld at their proper time.

"The moon will change its laws, and not be seen at its proper time. But in those days it will be seen in heaven, on top of a great chariot in the west. It will shine more than light should shine. Many leaders of the stars will wander off, change their ways and actions. Those will not appear at their proper times which have been prescribed for them, and all the classes of the stars will be shut up against wrongdoers. The thoughts of the inhabitants of the earth will go astray concerning them, and they will go astray from their ways. They will do wrong, and think themselves gods, and evil will increase among them. Punishment will come on them and destroy them."

## Enoch's Letter to Methuselah

## 81:1-10.

He said to me, "Enoch, look at the heavenly tablets and read what is written in it, and understand every individual fact."

Then I looked at everything that was written, and read everything that was written and understood it all, all the works of humankind, and of all the humans on earth for all generations of the world. Then I immediately blessed the Lord, the splendid king, because he made all the world's works. I praised the Lord because of his patience, and I blessed him because of the world's humans. At that time I said, "Blessed is the person who will die just and good, and against whom no record of crime has been recorded, and against whom no felony has been found."

Then those three sacred ones brought me and placed me on the earth, in front of the door of my house. They said to me, "Explain everything to Methuselah your son, and inform all your children, that no flesh will be acceptable in the Lord's presence, for he is their creator. We will leave you with your children for one year, until you recover your strength, so that you may instruct your family, write these things, and explain them to all your children. But in the second year they will take you from their midst and your heart will be strong. For the chosen will point out justice to the chosen, the just will celebrate with the just, congratulating each other, but the wrongdoers will die with wrongdoers and the traitor will be drowned with the traitor. Those who act justly will die on account of the works of humans, and will be collected because of the works of the wicked."

In those days they finished conversing with me, and I returned to my fellows, blessing the Lord of worlds.


## The Regulations of the Stars


**82:1-20**.

Now, my son Methuselah, I am telling you all these things and writing them down for you. I have revealed everything to you, and have given you books about all these things. My son Methuselah, preserve the books written by your father, so that you may reveal them to future generations. I have given wisdom to you, to your children, and your descendants, so that they may reveal to their children, for generations, this wisdom that is beyond their thinking. Those who understand it will not sleep, but hear it with their ears in order to learn this wisdom, and it will be considered better than eating this good food.

Blessed are all the just, blessed are all who behave in a just manner, in whom no crime is found, as in wrongdoers. In the numbering of all the days in which the sun progresses through heaven, it goes in and out of each portal for thirty days, with the leaders of the thousands of classes of the stars, together with the four which are added, and which divide the four quarters of the year, which lead them, and accompany them for four days. Because of these, people very much get it wrong, and do not calculate them in the calculation of the whole year, for they very much get it wrong in respect of them, for they do not know this accurately. But indeed these do belong in the calculation of the whole year, and are recorded forever, one in the first portal, one in the third, one in the fourth, and one in the sixth, and the year is completed in 364 days.

It has been accurately calculated and recorded. Uriel has explained to me, and communicated to me, about the luminaries, the months, the fixed times, the years, and the days. The Lord of all creation, on my account, commanded, according to the might of heaven, and the power which it possesses by day and night, Uriel to explain to people the laws of light, of the sun, moon, and stars, and of all the heavenly powers, which revolve with their respective orbs.

This is the regulation of the stars, which set in their places, in their seasons, in their times, in their days, and in their months. These are the names of those who lead them, who watch that they enter at their times, according to their regulation, in their months, in the times of their influence, and in their stations.

Their four leaders, who separate the four quarters of the year, enter first. After these, twelve leaders of their classes, who divide the months and the year into 364 days, with the leaders of a thousand, who divide the days, and for the four additional ones, there are leaders which divide the four quarters of the year.

These leaders of a thousand are in the midst of the leaders, and the leaders are added each behind a station, and their leaders make the division. These are the names of the leaders, who divide the four quarters of the year, which are appointed: Milkiel, Heeammelek, Melejal, and Narel. The names of those who lead them are Adnarel, Ijasusael, and Elomeel. These are the three who follow the leaders of the classes of stars, each following after the three leaders of the classes, which in turn follow after the leaders of the stations, who divide the four quarters of the year. In the first part of the year Melkejal rises and rules, this is named the southern sun. All the days of his influence, during which he rules, are 91 days.

And these are the signs of the days which are seen on earth in the days of his influence: sweat, heat, and calm. All the trees become fruitful, the leaf of every tree buds, the grain is harvested, the rose and every species of flower blossoms in the field, and the trees of winter wither. These are the names of the leaders who are under them: Berkael, Zelebsel, and another additional leader of a thousand is named Hilujaseph, the days of whose influence have come to an end. The next leader after them is Helemmelek, whose name they call the splendid sun, and all the days of his light are 91 days. These are the signs of the days on earth, heat and drought, while the trees bring forth their fruits, ripe and prepared, and produce their harvest. The flocks breed and bear young. All the fruits of the earth are harvested, with everything in the fields, and the winepress. This takes place during the time of his influence.

These are their names and orders, and the leaders who are chiefs of a thousand: Gidaijal, Keel, and Heel. And the name of the additional leader of a thousand is Asfael. The days of his influence are at an end.


## Enoch's First Vision


### 83:1-11.

And now I will show you, my son Methuselah, every sight which I saw prior to your birth. I will relate another vision, which I saw before I was married, they do not resemble each other. The first was when I was learning to write and the other before I married your mother. I saw a terrible vision, and sought the Lord about it. I was lying down in the house of my grandfather Mahalalel, when I saw in a vision the heavens collapse and they were snatched away and fell to the earth. I also saw the earth absorbed by a huge abyss, and mountains suspended over mountains. Hills were sinking on hills, and tall trees were gliding off from their trunks, and were being hurled into the abyss.

Words fell into my mouth and I cried out, "The earth is destroyed!"

Then my grandfather Mahalalel woke me up as I lay near him, and asked me, "Why did you cry out like this, my son, why are you moaning?"

I told him the whole vision which I had seen. He said to me, "My son, you have seen a terrible thing! The vision in your dream concerns every secret wrongdoing of the earth. It will sink into the abyss, and a great destruction will take place. Now, my son, get up, and implore the splendid Lord, for you are faithful, that a remnant may be left on the earth and that he would not completely destroy it. My son, all this disaster on earth comes down from heaven, and great destruction will come on the earth."

Then I got up, prayed, and pleaded, and wrote down my prayer for the generations of the world, explaining everything to my son Methuselah. When I had gone down below, and looked up to heaven, I saw the sun rising in the east, the moon setting in the west, a few scattered stars, and everything which God has known from the beginning, I blessed the Lord of judgment, and praised him, because he had sent the sun from the windows of the east, so that it rose and set and in the face of the heavens, and kept on the pathway appointed for it.

## 84:1-6.

I lifted up my hands with justice, and blessed the sacred, and the Great One. I spoke with the breath of my mouth, and with a mortal tongue, which God has formed for all the mortal humans, so that they may speak, giving them breath, a mouth, and a tongue to converse with. "Blessed are you, Lord, the King, great and powerful in your greatness, Lord of all the creatures of heaven, King of kings, God of the whole world, whose reign, kingdom, and magnificence last for ever and ever. Your dominion lasts for generation after generation. All the heavens are your throne forever, and the whole earth your footstool for ever and for ever. For you have made them, and you reign over everything. No deed whatsoever is beyond your power. Your wisdom is never changes, nor does it leave your throne or your presence. You know, see, and hear all things; there is nothing that is concealed from you, for you perceive everything.

"The angels of your heavens have misbehaved, and your fury will remain on mortal flesh, until the day of the great judgment. Now then, God, Lord and great King, I entreat you, and implore you to grant my prayer, that a posterity may be left for me on earth, and that the whole human race may not perish, so that the earth will not be left without inhabitants in the face of eternal destruction. My Lord, let the race which has made you angry perish from the earth, but establish a just and honest race for a posterity forever. Lord, do not ignore your servant's prayer!"

## Prophecy About the Animals

**85:1-9**.

After this I saw another dream, and I will explain it all to you, my son. Enoch arose and said to his son Methuselah, "My son, will I speak to you. Hear my words, and listen to the visionary dream of your father. Before I married your mother Edna, I saw a vision in my sleep. A cow (*Adam*) (*49*) sprung out of the earth, and this cow was white. After that a female young cow (*Eve*) sprung out, and other young cows were with it. One of them was black (*Cain*), and one was red (*Abel*). The black young cow (*Cain*) then struck the red one (*Abel*), and chased it over the earth.

"From then on I could see nothing more of the red young cow (*Abel*), but the black one (*Cain*) increased in size, and a female young cow (*his wife*) went with him. After this I saw many cows coming out (*their children*), looking like him and following him. The first female young cow (*Eve*) also went away from the first cow (*Adam*), and looked for the red young cow (*Abel*), but did not find him. She was greatly distressed while she was looking for him.

"Then I watched until the first cow (*Adam*) came to her and calmed her down, and she stopped crying. Afterwards she calved another white cow (*Seth*), and afterwards calved many cows and black young cows (*more children*). In my sleep I also perceived the white bull (*Seth*), which grew in the same way, and became a large white bull. After him many white cows (*his descendants*) which looked like him came out. They began to calve many other white cows (*his descendants*), which looked like them and followed each other."

**86:1-6**.

Again I looked attentively in my sleep, and surveyed heaven above. And a single star (*Azazel*) fell from heaven! It got up, and ate and grazed among those cows. After that I perceived the large black

86

cows, and all of them changed their stalls and their young cows, and they began to moan one with another!

Again I looked in my vision, and saw heaven, when I saw many stars (*The Watchers*), which descended, and projected themselves from heaven to where the first star (*Azazel*) was! It was the middle of those young cows and cows (*women and men*), grazing among them. I observed them, and they all acted like stallions ready to serve, and began to mount the young cows (*women*), all of whom became pregnant, and gave birth to elephants, camels, and donkeys! (*Giants, Nephilim, and Elioud.*) The cows were alarmed and terrified at this, and began biting with their teeth, devouring, and goring with their horns. And thus they began to eat those cows. All the inhabitants of the earth were terrified, shook with fear at them, and fled away!

## 87:1-4.

Again I perceived them, how they began to strike and gore each other, and the earth cried out. Then I lifted my eyes a second time to heaven, and saw in the vision that there came from heaven, beings that looked like white humans. Four (*Archangels*) came from there, and three (*angels*) with them. Those three, who came out last, took me by my hand and lifted me from the races of earth, and lifted me to a high place. Then they showed me a tower high above the earth, with all the hills much lower. One said to me, "Stay here, until you see what happens to those elephants, camels, and donkeys (*Giants, Nephilim and Elioud*), to the stars (*the Watchers*), and to all the cows (*the humans*).

## 88:1-3.

Then I looked at the one of the four white humans, who came out first (*Raphael*). He seized the first star (*Azazel*) which had fallen from heaven. He bound it hand and foot and threw it into an abyss, a narrow, deep, terrible, and gloomy abyss. Then one of them drew his sword, and gave it to the elephants, camels, and donkeys (*Giants, Nephilim and Elioud*), who began to strike each other. And the whole earth shook because of them. And when I looked in the vision, one of those four who had come out threw a line from heaven, and collected all the huge stars, whose penises were like those of horses, and bound them all hand and foot, and threw them into an abyss of the earth.

## 89:1-78.

Then one of those four went to a white cow (*Noah*), and taught him a mystery and he was trembling. He was born a bull, and became a human, and he built a large vessel (*the Ark*). He lived in it, and three cows (*Shem, Ham and Japheth*) lived with him in that vessel, which covered them.

Again I lifted up my eyes towards heaven, and saw a high roof. Seven channels were above it, and they poured much water on a certain place. Again I looked, and there springs opened on the earth in that large place! The water began to bubble up, and rose over the earth, so that the place was not seen, and all its soil was covered with water. There was much water over it, darkness, and clouds. I looked at the height of this water, and it was higher than the place. It flowed over the place, and stood higher than the earth. Then all the cows (*humans*) which were gathered there, while I looked on them, were drowned, swallowed up, and destroyed in the water. But the vessel (*the Ark*) floated above it. All the cows, the elephants, the camels, and the donkeys (*humans, Giants, Nephilim and Elioud*), were drowned on the earth, along with all the animals, so that I could not see them. They were unable to get out, but perished and sank into the deep.

Again I looked in the vision until those water channels were removed from that high roof, and the fountains of the earth became level, while other depths were opened. The water began to go down into them, until dry ground appeared. The vessel (*the Ark*) settled on the earth, the darkness receded, and it became light. Then the white cow (*Noah*) which became a human went out of the ship and the three cows (*Shem, Ham, and Japheth*) with him. One of the three cows was white, resembling that cow, one of them was red as blood, and one of them was black (*different human races*). And the white cow (*Noah*) left them. They began to produce wild animals and birds, so from them came different species: lions, tigers, wolves, dogs, hyenas, wild boars, foxes, squirrels, swine, falcons, vultures, kites, eagles, and ravens. Then the white cow (*Abraham*) was born amongst them. And they began to bite each other, when the white cow (*Abraham*), which was born among them, fathered a wild donkey (*Ishmael*) and a white bull (*Isaac*) at the same time, and after that many wild donkeys (*the Ishmaelites*). Then the white cow, (*Isaac*) which was born, gave birth to a black wild sow and a white sheep (*Esau and Jacob*).

That wild sow also fathered many swine. And that sheep (*Jacob*) fathered twelve sheep (*The Twelve Patriarchs*). When those twelve sheep grew up, they handed one of them (*Joseph*) to the donkeys (*the Midianites*) and they handed that sheep (*Joseph*) to the wolves (*the Egyptians*), and he grew up among them. Then the Lord brought the eleven other sheep (*the remaining Patriarchs*), to live and graze with him in the middle of the wolves (*the Egyptians*). They increased, and became many flocks of sheep (*had many descendants*). But the wolves (*the Egyptians*) began to frighten them and oppress them, until they took off with their young ones. And they left their young (*the Egyptians' young*) in currents of deep water.

Now the sheep (*the Hebrews*) began to cry out because of their young, and complained to their Lord. One (*Moses*) which had been saved from the wolves (*the Egyptians*), escaped, and went away to the wild donkeys (*the Ishmaelites*). I saw the sheep (*the Hebrews*) moaning, crying, and petitioning their Lord with all their might, until the Lord of the sheep descended in response to their call from his high dwelling, went to them, and inspected them. He called that sheep (*Moses*) which had left the wolves (*the Egyptians*), and told him to make the wolves (*the Egyptians*) understand that they were not to touch the sheep (the Hebrews). Then that sheep (*Moses*) went to the wolves (*the Egyptians*) with the Lord's words, when another sheep (*Aaron*) met him and went with him.

Both of them together entered the dwelling of the wolves (*the Egyptians*), and spoke to them to make them understand that from then on they were not to touch the sheep (*the Hebrews*). Afterwards I saw how the wolves (*the Egyptians*) were acting even more forcefully to the sheep (*the Hebrews*) with all their might. The sheep (*the Hebrews*) cried out, and their Lord came to them. He began to strike the wolves (*the Egyptians*), who began to moan, but the sheep (*the Hebrews*) kept quiet and from then on did not call out. I then watched them until they left the wolves (the Egyptians). The eyes of the wolves (*the Egyptians*) were blinded, and they went out and pursued sheep (*the Hebrews*) with all their might. But the Lord of the sheep went with them and guided them. All his sheep followed him.

His face was terrifying and splendid, and his appearance was superlative. Yet the wolves (*the Egyptians*) began to chase the sheep (*the Hebrews*), until they overtook them in a certain body of water (*The Red Sea*). Then that water became divided, the water standing up on both sides in front of them. And while their Lord was guiding them, he placed himself between them and the wolves (*the Egyptians*). The wolves (*the Egyptians*) however had not yet seen the sheep (*the Hebrews*), but went into the middle of the water after them into the body of water (*The Red Sea*). But when they saw the Lord of the sheep, they turned to flee from him. Then the water returned, and suddenly went back to its natural state. It became full, and swelled up until it covered the wolves (*the Egyptians*). And I saw that all the wolves (*the Egyptians*) which had followed the sheep (*the Hebrews*) perished and drowned.

But the sheep (*the Hebrews*) passed over this water, and went to a wilderness, which was without both water and grass. And they began to open their eyes and see. Then I saw the Lord of the sheep inspecting them, and giving them water and grass. The sheep (*Moses*) already mentioned was going with them and guiding them. And when he had ascended the top of a tall rock, the Lord of the sheep sent him to them. Afterwards I saw their Lord standing in front them, and his face was terribly severe. When they all saw him, they were frightened by his appearance. All of them were alarmed, and trembled. They cried out after that sheep (*Moses*), and to the other sheep (*the Hebrews*) who had been with him, and who was in among them, "We are unable to stand in our Lord's presence, or look at him!"

Then that sheep (*Moses*) who guided them went away, and ascended the top of the rock (*Mount Sinai*). Then the rest of the sheep (*the Hebrews*) began to grow blind, and to wander from the pathway that had been shown them, but he was unaware of it. Their Lord however was extremely angry with them, and when that sheep (*Moses*) had learned what had happened, he came down from the top of the rock (*Mount Sinai*), and coming to the sheep (*the Hebrews*), found that there were many which had become blind, and had wandered off the path. As soon as they saw him, they were afraid and trembled and wanted to return to their pens.

Then that sheep (*Moses*), taking with him other sheep (*Hebrews*), went to those which had gone astray and began to kill them. They were terrified by his appearance. Then he caused those which had gone astray to come back, and they went back to their pens. I also saw there in the vision, that this sheep who became a man (*Moses*), built a house (*the desert Tabernacle*) for the Lord of the sheep, and made them all stand in the house. I looked until the sheep (*Hebrews*) which had met this sheep, their guide (*Moses*), died. I also looked until all the large sheep perished, while smaller ones rose up in their place, and came to grazing land, and approached a river of water (*The River Jordan*).

Then that sheep, their guide, who became a human (*Moses*), separated from them and died. All the sheep missed him, and cried for him bitterly. I also watched until they stopped crying for that sheep (*Moses*), and passed over the river of water (*The River Jordan*). And there arose other sheep (*The Judges of Israel*), all of whom guided them, instead of those who had previously conducted them but who now were dead. Then I watched until the sheep (*the Hebrews*) came to a good place, a luscious and magnificent land (*Canaan*). I saw also that they became satisfied, that their house (*the Tabernacle*) was in the middle of them in a wonderful land. Sometimes their eyes were opened, and sometimes they were blind, until another sheep (*Samuel*) arose and guided them. He brought them all back, and their eyes were opened.

Then dogs, foxes, and wild boars began to devour the sheep (*the Hebrews*), until again another sheep (*Saul*) arose, the master of the flock, one of themselves, a ram (*Saul*), to guide them. This ram (*Saul*) began to butt on every side those dogs (*the Philistines*), foxes, and wild boars, until they all perished. The eyes of the sheep were opened, and saw the ram (*Saul*) in the middle of the sheep (*Hebrews*), how it had abandoned its splendor, and had begun to strike the sheep (*Hebrews*), trampling them, and behaving without decorum. Then their Lord sent the former sheep (*Samuel*) again to a different sheep (*David*), and raised him up to be a ram, and to guide them instead of that sheep (*Saul*) which had abandoned its splendor. That sheep went to him (*David*) and speaking with him alone, raised up that ram, and made him a prince and leader of the flock (*Hebrews*).

All the time that the dogs (*the Philistines*) troubled the sheep, the first ram (*Saul*) paid respect to this latter ram (*David*). Then the latter ram (*David*) got up and fled away from him. And I saw that those dogs (*the Philistines*) caused the first ram (*Saul*) to fall. But the latter ram (*David*) arose, and guided the smaller sheep (*the Hebrews*). That ram (*David*) likewise fathered many sheep, and then died. Then there was a smaller sheep (*Solomon*), which became a ram (*king*) instead of him, a prince and leader, guiding the flock (*Hebrews*). And the sheep (*Hebrews*) grew and increased in number. And all the dogs (*the Philistines*), foxes, and wild boars were afraid, and ran away from him. That ram (*Solomon*) also struck and killed all the wild animals, so that they could not again triumph over the sheep (*Hebrews*), nor at any time ever snatch anything from them.

And that house was made large and wide, and a high tower (*Temple*) was built on it for the sheep (*Hebrews*), for the Lord of the sheep. The house was low, but the tower (*Temple*) was elevated and very high. Then the Lord of the sheep stood on the high tower (*Temple*), and they spread a full table to in front of him. Again I saw those sheep (*Hebrews*) who went astray, and went various ways, and abandoned that their house. The Lord of the sheep called some of the sheep (*Hebrews*) among them, whom he sent to the sheep (*prophets*), but the sheep (*the Hebrews*) began to kill them. But one of them (*Elijah*) was saved from slaughter. He sprang up and cried out against the sheep (*the Hebrews*) who wanted to kill him. But the Lord of the sheep saved him from them, and brought it up to me, and made it stay. He also sent many others to them (*prophets*), to bear witness, and to complain about them. Again I saw, when some of them abandoned the house of their Lord, and his tower (*Temple*), they went astray with everything, and their eyes were blinded. I saw that the Lord of the sheep did much slaughter among them in their pasture, until they invited that slaughter, and betrayed his place. Then he handed them over to lions, tigers, wolves, hyenas, to the power of foxes, and to all animals (*all human races*).

And the wild animals began to tear the sheep (*Hebrews*). I also saw that he abandoned the house of their ancestors (*the Levites took the Ark*), and their tower (*Temple*), and handed them over to the power of lions (*the Assyrians*) to tear them up and devour them, and handed them over to the power of all animals (*all human races*). Then I began to cry out with all my might, pleading with the Lord of the sheep, and showing him how the sheep (*Hebrews*) were devoured by all the animals. But he looked on in silence, happy that they were devoured, swallowed up, and carried away, and leaving them in the power of all the animals (*all human races*) for food.

He called also seventy shepherds, and designated the care of the sheep (*the Hebrews*) to them, that they would care for them. He said to them and to their associates, "Every one of you from now on is to take care of the sheep (*the Hebrews*), and you are to do whatever I order you to do, and I will hand them over to you properly numbered. I will tell you which of them is to be slain, and you are to destroy these ones." And he handed the sheep over to them.

Then he called another, and said, "Observe, and watch everything that the shepherds do to these sheep, because many more of them than I have commanded will be destroyed. Make an account of every excess of slaughter which the shepherds commit, of how many have perished by my order, and how many they may have destroyed by their own decision. There will be an account of all the destruction brought about by each of the shepherds, and according to the number, I will have a record made for evidence as to how many they have destroyed by their own decision, and how many they have handed over for destruction. This is so that I may have this evidence against them, and so that I may know all their dealings, and that I may see what they will do in handing the sheep over to them, whether or not they will act as I have ordered them.

"However, they are to be unaware of this. You are not to make any explanation to them, and you are not to reprimand them, but there will be an account of all the destruction done by each individual in their respective times."

Then they began to kill, and destroy more than they were ordered to. They left the sheep (*Hebrews*) in the power of the lions (*the Assyrians*), so that very many of them were eaten and swallowed up by lions and tigers, and wild boars preyed on them.

They burnt that tower (*Temple*), and overthrew that house. Then I was extremely upset because of the tower (*Temple*), and because the house of the sheep was overthrown. Afterwards I was unable to perceive whether they entered that house again. The shepherds and their associates handed them over to all the wild animals, so that they could eat them. Each of them in their own time, according to their number, was delivered up, and it was recorded in a book how each of them was destroyed. However, more than ordered were killed and destroyed. Then I began to cry, and I was extremely upset because of the sheep.

In the same way too I saw in the vision the one who wrote, how daily he wrote down each one destroyed by the shepherds. He brought up and showed each of his books to the Lord of the sheep. His books contained everything they had done, and everything each of them had made away with, and everything which they had handed over to be destroyed. The Lord of the sheep took the book up in his hands, read it, sealed it, and put it down.

After this, I saw shepherds pasturing sheep for twelve hours. And three of the sheep (*Ezra, Haggai, and Zechariah*) returned (*the return after exile*), arrived, went in, and began building everything that had fallen from that house! But the wild boars (*the Samaritans*) tried to prevent them, but they were not able to. Again they began to build as before, and raised up that tower, which was a high tower (*the second Temple*). And again they began to place a table in front of the tower (*the second Temple*) which had every impure and unclean kind of food on it. In addition to this, all the sheep were blinded and could not see, as was also the case with the shepherds. Thus they handed more over to the shepherds to be destroyed, and they trampled them underfoot and ate them up.

Yet their Lord stayed silent, until all the sheep were all mixed with the wild animals, but the shepherds did not save them from the power of the wild animals. Then he who wrote the book went up and showed it, and read it out at the residence of the Lord of the sheep. He petitioned him for them, and prayed, pointing out every act of the shepherds, and testifying against them all in his presence. Then he took the book, and deposited it with their Lord, and left.


**90:1-42**.

I looked until the time that 35 shepherds were pasturing the sheep in the same way as the first shepherds. Others then received them into their hands to pasture them in their respective times, each shepherd in his own time. Afterwards I saw in the vision that all the birds of sky arrived, eagles, vultures, kites, and ravens. The eagles (*the Romans*) led them all. They began to devour the sheep, to peck out their eyes, and to eat up their bodies. The sheep cried out because their bodies were devoured by the birds. I also cried out, and groaned in my sleep because of the shepherd which pastured the flock.

And I looked, while the sheep were eaten up by the dogs, by the eagles, and by the kites. They did not leave them flesh or skin, or their muscles, until only their bones remained, until their bones fell on the ground. And the sheep became few. I also observed during that time that 23 shepherds were pasturing, and they completed, each in their time, 58 times. Then small lambs were born from those white sheep, and they began to open their eyes and see, crying out to the sheep. The sheep, however, did not cry out to them, nor did they hear what they said to them, but they were deaf, blind, and stubborn to the utmost. I saw in the vision that ravens flew down on those lambs, and took one of them, and tore the sheep in pieces, and devoured them. I watched until horns grew on those lambs, and that the ravens knocked down their horns. I also saw that a large horn sprouted out on one of the sheep, and their eyes were opened. He looked at them and their eyes were opened. He called out to them and they ran to him.

And besides this, all the eagles, the vultures, the ravens and the kites were still carrying off the sheep, flying down on them and devouring them. The sheep were silent, but the rams lamented and called out. Then the ravens battled and grappled with them. They wished to break his horn, but they did not triumph over him. I looked on until the shepherds, the eagles, the vultures, and the kites came and called out to the ravens to break the horn of the ram, to fight him and kill him. But he struggled with them, and called out for help.

Then I watched until that man, who had written down the names of the shepherds, and who had ascended into the Lord of the sheep's presence, arrived. He brought assistance, and showed the ram that help was on its way. I also watched until the Lord of the sheep came to them angrily, while all those who saw him fled away, all fell down in his presence. All the eagles, the vultures, ravens, and kites assembled, and brought with them all the wild sheep. They all came together and tried to break the ram's horn. Then I saw that the man, who wrote the book at the order of the Lord, opened the book of destruction that the last twelve shepherds had made. He pointed out in the presence of the Lord of the sheep that they had destroyed more than had those who preceded them.

I saw also that the Lord of the sheep came to them, and took the scepter of his anger in his hand. He struck the earth, which split open. All the animals and birds of the sky fell from the sheep and sunk into the earth, which closed over them. I also saw that a large sword was given to the sheep, and they went out against all the wild animals to kill them. All the beasts and birds of the sky fled from them.

I watched until a throne was erected in a lovely land. The Lord of the sheep sat on it. They took all the sealed books and opened them in front of him. Then the Lord called the first seven white ones, and commanded them to bring before him the first (*Azazel*) of the first stars, which preceded the stars whose penises were like horses, and they brought them all before him. And he spoke to the man who wrote in his presence, who was one of the seven white ones, "Take those seventy shepherds, to whom I handed over the sheep, and who killed more of them than I ordered."

I saw them all bound, and standing in front of him. The judgment was held, first on the stars (*The Watchers*), which were judged and found guilty, and they went to the place of punishment. They were thrown into a deep place which was full of flaming fire, and full of pillars of fire. Then the seventy shepherds were judged and found guilty, and they were thrown into the fiery abyss. At that time I also saw that one abyss was opened in the middle of the earth which was full of fire. The blind sheep were brought there, and were judged and found guilty, and were thrown into that abyss of fire on the earth, and burnt. The abyss was on the right side of that house. And I saw the sheep burning, and their bones dissolving.

I stood watching him folding up that ancient house, and they removed all its pillars and all the beams and ornaments in it. They removed it and put it in a place on the right side of the earth. I also saw that the Lord of the sheep produced a new house, bigger and taller than the former, and he set it up on the site of the first one which had been folded up. All its pillars were new, and its ornaments were new and more plentiful than the former ancient one, which had been removed, and all the sheep were in it. All the beasts of the earth, and all the birds of heaven, fell down and worshipped them, petitioning them, and obeying them in everything. And the Lord of the sheep was in the middle of it. And I saw all the sheep that were left, all the animals of the earth, and all the birds of the sky, falling down and worshipping those sheep, and begging them and obeying their every command.

Then those three, who were dressed in white, and who had taken hold of my hand, the ones who had previously caused me to ascend, and with the hand of him who spoke holding me, raised me up, and placed me among the sheep, before the judgment took place. The sheep were all white and their wool was long and pure. Then all who had perished and had been destroyed, all the wild animals, and every bird of the sky, assembled in that house, while the Lord of the sheep celebrated greatly because they were all good, and had returned to his dwelling.

And I watched until they put down the sword which had been given to the sheep, and returned it to his house, sealing it up in the Lord's presence. All the sheep were enclosed in that house, but it was not capable of containing them, and the eyes of all of them were opened. There was not one among them who did not see. I also saw that the house was large, wide, and extremely full. I also saw that a white cow was born, and its horns were big, and that all the wild animals, and all the birds of the sky, were afraid of it, and continually begged him.

Then I saw that the nature of all of them was changed, and that they became white cows. The first among them was a lamb. It was large and on its head were large black horns. While the Lord of the sheep celebrated about them and about all the cows, I lay down among them. I woke up and saw everything. This is the vision which I saw when I was asleep. I woke up and blessed the just Lord, and praised him. Afterwards I cried profusely, and my tears did not stop, until I could no longer stand it. While I was looking, they flowed on account of what I saw, for everything will come to pass and be fulfilled, all the deeds of humankind in their order were seen by me. That night I remembered my previous dream, and so I cried and I was troubled, because I had seen that vision.

**Prophecy of the Ten Weeks**

**91:1-19.**

And now, my son Methuselah, call all your siblings to me, and assemble your mother's children for me, for a voice calls me, and a spirit is poured out on me, so that I may show you everything which will happen to you forever. Then Methuselah went and called all his siblings to him, and gathered his relatives. He spoke to all his children truthfully, and said, "My children, hear every word of your father, and listen properly to the voice of my mouth, as I wish to have your attention while I address you. My beloved, have integrity, and behave justly! Do not approach integrity in a deceitful way, and do not associate with deceitful people, but behave justly, my children, and this will guide you in good pathways, and truth will be your companion.

"For I know that oppression will continue and prevail on the earth and that great punishment will in the end take place on earth, and all wrongdoing will come to an end. It will be cut off from its root, and its whole structure will pass away. However wrongdoing will be renewed, and completed on earth. Every criminal act, and every act of oppression and wickedness, will prevail a second time. So then when injustice, wrongdoing, blasphemy, tyranny, and every evil work increase, and when wrongdoing, impiety, and uncleanness increase, then great punishment be inflicted on them all from heaven.

"The sacred Lord will go out angrily, and great punishment will be inflicted on them all from heaven. The sacred Lord will go out angrily, in order to execute judgment on earth. In those days oppression will be cut off from its roots, and iniquity with fraudulent crime will be destroyed from under heaven. Every strong place will be surrendered with its inhabitants, and burnt with fire. They will be brought from every part of the earth, and be cast into a fiery judgment. They will perish by being angrily overpowered forever. Justice will be raised up from sleep, and wisdom will get up and be given to them. Then the roots of wrongdoing will be cut off, wrongdoers and blasphemers will perish by the sword. And now, my children, I will describe and point out to you the pathway of justice and the pathway of oppression. I will point them out to you again, so that you may know what is to come. Listen to me now, my children, and behave

98

justly! Do not behave in an oppressive way, for all who behave wickedly will perish for ever."

## 92:1-5.

That which was written by Enoch. He wrote this complete instruction of wisdom which is praised by people and a judge of the whole earth, for all my children who will live on earth, and for subsequent generations who will conduct themselves in a just and peaceful manner. Do not let your inner self worry on account of the times, for the sacred Great One has prescribed a time for all things.

The just one will awake from sleep, will arise, and proceed along the way of justice, in all its pathways which will be good and compassionate forever. He will be compassionate to the just person, and give them integrity and power forever. He will behave well and justly forever, and will walk in eternal light, but wrongdoing will perish in eternal darkness, and from that time on will never be seen again.

## 93:1-14.

After this, Enoch began to speak from a book. Enoch said, "About the just people, about the chosen of the world, and about the plant of justice and integrity, about these things will I speak, and these things will I explain to you, my children, I, Enoch, according to that which has been shown to me, from my heavenly vision and from the words of the sacred angels (50) and understanding from the tablet of heaven."

Enoch then began to speak from a book, and said, "I was born the seventh, in the first week, while judgment and justice waited patiently. But after me, in the second week, great wickedness will arise, and fraud will spring out. In that week the end of the first will happen, in which humankind will be safe. But when the first week comes to an end, wrongdoing will spring up, and during the second week he will execute the decree on wrongdoers. Then after that, at the end of the third week, a just person will be selected as the plant of just judgment, and after him the just plant will come forever.

"Then after that, at the end of the fourth week, the visions of the sacred and the just will be seen, and the law of generation after generation, and a living place will be made for them. Then after that, at the end of the fifth week, the splendid and masterful house will be erected forever. Then after that, in the sixth week, all those who are in it will be darkened, and the hearts of all of them will forget wisdom. In it, a person will get up and come out. At its end he will burn the masterful house with fire, and the whole race of the chosen root will be dispersed.

"Then after that, in the seventh week, a rebellious generation will arise. It will do many rebellious deeds. At its end, the just will be selected from the eternal just plant, and they will be given seven portions of the teaching of his whole creation. Then after that, there will be another week, the eighth of justice, and a sword will be given to execute judgment and justice on all oppressors. Wrongdoers will be handed over to the just, and at its end they will acquire dwellings because they are just, and the dwelling of the splendid great king will be established forever. Then after that, in the ninth week, the just judgment will be revealed to the whole world. All the deeds of the ungodly will disappear from the whole earth, the world will be marked for destruction, and all people will look for the just pathway.

"And after this, on the seventh day of the tenth week, there will be an eternal judgment that will be executed on the Watchers, and a spacious eternal heaven will spring out amongst the angels. The former heaven will vanish and pass away, and a new heaven will appear, and all the heavenly powers will shine forever with seven times the light. Afterwards there will be many weeks, which will exist forever with integrity and justice. From then on wrongdoing will not be named there for ever and ever.

"Who of all the humans is capable of hearing the voice of the Sacred One without emotion? Who is capable of thinking his thoughts? Who is capable of understanding all the workings of heaven? Who is capable of understanding the actions of heaven? They may see its workings, but not how it works. They may be capable of speaking about it, but not of ascending to it. They may see all the boundaries of these things, and think on them, but not understand them. What human is able to understand the breadth and length of the earth? And to whom have all its measurements been shown? Is any human capable of understanding the extent of heaven, what its height is, and by what it is supported, or the numbers of the stars, and where all the luminaries rest?"

## Enoch's Message

### 94:1-11.

Now, my children, let me urge you to love justice, and to behave justly, for the pathways of justice are worthy to be accepted, but the paths of wickedness will suddenly fail and fade away. To certain people of a future generation the pathways of oppression and death will be revealed, but they keep far away from them, and will not follow them. Now I urge you who are just, not to behave in an evil or oppressive manner, or in a manner which causes death. Do not approach these pathways so that you will not be destroyed. And choose for yourselves justice, and a good life. Walk along the peaceful pathways, so that you may live and be found worthy. Keep my words in your innermost thoughts, and do not let them leave your hearts, for I know that wrongdoers cunningly advise people to commit crimes. No place will be found for wisdom, and wrongdoing will increase. Woe to those who build evildoing and oppression, as they will suddenly be undermined, and will never find peace. Woe to those who build up their houses with wrongdoing, for from their very foundations they will be demolished, and they themselves will fall by the sword. Those who acquire gold and silver will justly and suddenly be destroyed in the judgment. Woe to you who are rich, for you have trusted your riches, but your riches will be removed from you, because you have not remembered the Most High in the days of your prosperity.

You have committed blasphemy and wickedness, and are destined for the days of the outpouring of blood, for the day of darkness, and for the day of the great judgment. This I will declare and point out to you, that he who created you will destroy you, and when you fall, he will not show you any compassion, but your Creator will celebrate over your destruction. Your just ones in those days will be a reproach to the wrongdoers and the ungodly.

## 95:1-7.

If only my eyes were clouds of water, so that I might weep over you, and pour out my tears like rain, and rest from the sorrow of my heart! Who permitted you to hate and to do wrong? Judgment will come on you, you wrongdoers! The just will not fear the wicked, because God will give them over to your hands, so that you may avenge yourselves on them as you wish. Woe to you who pronounce curses that you cannot remove; healing will be far removed from you because of your wrongdoings! Woe to you who repay your neighbor with evil, for you will be repaid according to your actions! Woe to you, false witnesses, you who do evil, for you will suddenly perish! Woe to you, wrongdoers, for you persecute the just, for you yourselves will be handed over and maltreated, and their yoke will be heavy on you!

## 96:1-8.

Be hopeful, you just, for wrongdoers will suddenly perish in front of you, and you will exercise power over them, as you like. In the day of the sufferings of wrongdoers your offspring will be lifted up like eagles. Your nest will be higher than that of the vultures. You will go up, and enter the openings in the earth and the clefts of the rocks, forever, like the lawless, but they will groan and weep over you, like mountain goats. You will not be afraid of those who trouble you, for healing will be yours, a splendid light will shine around you, and the tranquil voice will be heard from heaven. Woe to you, wrongdoers, for your wealth makes you appear sacred, but your hearts prove you to be wrongdoers! This word will testify against you as a reminder of your crimes.

Woe to you who feed on the best of the grain, and drink the best of the deepest spring, and trample down the humble with your power! Woe to you who drink water when you wish to, for suddenly you will be repaid, worn out and withered, because you have left the foundation of life! Woe to you who act wickedly, deceitfully, and blasphemously, for there will be a reminder of evil against you! Woe to you, you powerful, you who powerfully strike down justice, for the day of your destruction will come, while at that time many good days will be the allotment of the just at the time of your judgment!

**97:1-10.**

Believe, you just ones, that wrongdoers will be disgraced, and perish in the day of judgment. You wrongdoers will be aware of it, for the Most High will remember your destruction, and the angels will celebrate it. What will you do, you wrongdoers? And where will you flee in the day of judgment when you hear the words of the just prayer? You are not like those against whom this word bears witness, "You are associates of wrongdoers!"

In those days the prayers of the just will come up in the Lord's presence and the day of your judgment will arrive, and every detail of your wrongdoing will be related in the presence of the great sacred one. Your faces will be covered with shame, while every deed founded on crime will be discarded. Woe to you, wrongdoers, who are in the middle of the sea, or on dry land, their memory will prove harmful to you! Woe to you who amass silver not obtained by honest means, and say, "Our barns are full, and our house's servants are as abundant as overflowing water."

Like water your life will pass away, for your wealth will not be permanent, but will suddenly leave you, because you have obtained it all dishonestly, and you will be handed over to extreme denunciation.

**98:1-16.**

And now I swear to you, the crafty, as well as the foolish, that you will see many things on the earth. You men will clothe yourselves more elegantly than a woman, and with more ornaments than a girl, dressing yourselves magnificently, ornamentally, powerfully, and in silver - but gold, purple, honor, and wealth flow away like water. Because of this, they do not have knowledge or wisdom. Thus they will perish because of this, together with their riches, all their splendor, and their honor, but their spirits will be thrown into a fiery furnace with disgrace, with slaughter, and in extreme poverty. I have sworn to you, you wrongdoers, that just as a mountain or hill has not been a woman's maid, nor was wrongdoing sent down to earth, but humans themselves created it, and those who commit it will be cursed.

Barrenness has not been inflicted on a woman, but because of her actions she will die childless. I swear to you, wrongdoers, by the sacred great one, that all your wrongdoings are revealed in heaven, and that none of your oppressive acts are hidden or secret. Don't let your inner self think, and don't say to yourself, that every crime is not clearly seen. In heaven it is written down daily in the presence of the Most High. From now on it will be made clear, for every wrongful act you commit will be recorded daily, until the time of your judgment.

Woe to you, you fools, for you will perish because of your foolishness! You will not listen to the wise, and you will not obtain anything good. So then now know that you are ready for the day of destruction. Have no hope that wrongdoers will live, but in the process of time you will die eventually, for you are not marked for ransom. Instead, you are destined for the day of the great judgment, for the day of distress, and the extreme shame of your lives. Woe to you who are stubborn, who commit crime, and feed on blood! From where do you feed on good things to eat and drink, and be satisfied? Is it not because our Lord, the Most High, has placed abundance on the earth? You will find no peace.

Woe to you who love wrongful acts! Why do you hope for good to happen to you? Know that you will be given over to the hands of the just ones, who will cut your throats and kill you, and will not show you any compassion. Woe to you who celebrate the troubles of the just, for a grave will not be dug for you! Woe to you who frustrate the words of the just, for there will be no hope of life for you! Woe to you who write down lying words, and the words of the wicked, for they record their lies, so that people will hear and not forget their foolishness! They will not find any peace, but they will certainly die suddenly.

## 99:1-16.

Woe to those who act wickedly, who praise and honor false words! You will be lost, and will not have a good life Woe to you who change truthful words! They contravene the eternal decree, and consider themselves not to be wrongdoers. They will be trampled down on the earth. You just ones, in those days you will be considered worthy to have your prayers rise up in remembrance. They

104

will have them put as evidence in front of the angels, so that they can record the wrongdoers' acts in the presence of the Most High.

In those days the nations will be overthrown, but the races of the nations will rise again in the day of destruction. In those days women who become pregnant will abort their children, and leave them. Their offspring will slip from them, and they will leave their nursing babies. They will never return to them, and will not show compassion to their loved ones. Again I swear to you, wrongdoers, that crime is ready for the day of blood which never ceases. They will worship stones, and carve golden, silver, wooden and clay images. Some, with no knowledge, will worship unclean spirits, demons, and all kinds of idols, in temples, but will get no help from them. They will become ungodly through their foolishness, and their eyes will be blinded through the fear in their hearts and through visions in their dreams. Through these they will become ungodly and fearful, lying in all their actions, and worshipping stones. They will be destroyed at the same time. But in those days blessed will be those who accept words of wisdom, and understand and follow the paths of the Most High, who behave justly, and who do not act wickedly with the wicked. They will be saved. Woe to you who extend crime to your neighbor, for you will be killed in Sheol!

Woe to you who lay the foundations of wrongdoing and deceit, and who cause bitterness on earth, because you will be consumed by it! Woe to you who build your houses by the labor of others, and construct them with the stones of crime, I tell you, you will not find peace! Woe to you who despise the extent of the eternal inheritance of your ancestors, and whose lives follow idols, for you there will be no peace! Woe to those who do wrong and help blasphemy, who kill their neighbor until the day of the great judgment, for he will throw down your splendor! You put evil in your hearts, and stir up the spirit of his anger and consequently he will destroy every one of you by the sword. Then all the just and the sacred will remember your crimes.

## 100:1-12.

In those days fathers will be struck down with their children in front of each other, and siblings will fall dead with their siblings until their blood flows like a river. For a man will not withhold his hand in mercy from his children, nor from his children's children - he will kill them. The wrongdoer will not restrain his hand from his honored brother. From the dawn of day to the setting of the sun they will kill each other. The horse will wade up to its chest, and the chariot will sink to its axle, in the blood of wrongdoers.

In those days the angels will come down into the hidden places, and collect in one spot all who have assisted in crime. On that day the Most High will rise up to execute the great judgment on all wrongdoers, and to set guards from the sacred angels, over all the just and sacred, that they may protect them like the apple of an eye, until every evil, and every crime is wiped out. Even though the just sleep a long sleep, they have nothing to fear. The wise will see the truth, and the inhabitants of the earth. (51) will understand every word of this book, knowing that their riches cannot save them or wipe out their crimes.

Woe to you, wrongdoers, when you afflict the just on the day of the great trouble, and burn them with fire, you will be paid back for your actions! Woe to you who have stubborn hearts, who watch in order to devise evil! You will be afraid and no one will help you. Woe to you, wrongdoers, for with the words of your mouths, and with the work of your hands, you have acted wickedly! You will be burnt in the flames of a blazing fire. And now know, that the angels will inquire into your conduct in heaven, from the sun, the moon, and the stars, will they inquire about your crimes, for on earth you execute judgment on the just. Every cloud, the snow, the dew, and the rain will bear witness against you, for all of them will be withheld from you so that they will not fall on you, and they will think about your crimes. Now then bring gifts to the rain so that it will not be withheld and will descend on you, and to the dew, which will fall on you if it has received gold and silver from you. But when the frost, snow, cold, every snowy wind, and all their irritations fall on you, in those days you will not be able to stand in front of them.

### 101:1-9.

Consider heaven, all you inhabitants of heaven, and all the works of the Most High, and respect him, and never do evil in his presence.

If he shut up the windows of heaven and withheld the rain and dew, so that it did not fall on the earth because of you, what will you do? And if he sends his anger on you and all your deeds, will you not appeal to him? You speak against his justice in arrogant and powerful language. To you there will be no peace.

Do you not see ships' captains, how their vessels are tossed about by the waves, torn to pieces by the winds, and exposed to the greatest danger? For this reason they are afraid, because all their possessions are at sea with them, and they only think negatively, because the sea may swallow them up, and they may perish in it. Is not the whole sea, all its waters, and all its movement, the work of the Most High, he who has sealed up all its workings, and girded it on every side with sand? Does it not dry up at his rebuke and become afraid, while all its fish and everything in it die? But you wrongdoers on the earth are not afraid of him. Is he not the maker of heaven and earth and of everything that is in them? And he who has given knowledge and wisdom to all things that move on the earth and in the sea? Don't the ships' captains fear the ocean? Yet wrongdoers are not afraid of the Most High.

## 102:1-11.

In those days, when he directs a severe fire at you, where will you flee, and where will you be safe? And when he sends his word against you, will you not be afraid and terrified? All the luminaries are shaken with great fear, and all the earth will be terrified, and will tremble and be anxious. All the angels will carry the commands they received, and will want to hide from the presence of the one who is greatly splendid, while the inhabitants of the earth are afraid and terrified. But you, wrongdoers, are accursed forever, you will not find peace.

Do not be afraid, souls of the just, but be hopeful, you who were just when you died. Do not grieve, because your souls descend to Sheol with sadness, and because in your lifetime your bodies did not receive a reimbursement in proportion to your goodness, but when you die the wrongdoers will say about you, "As we die, the just die. What use to them were their actions? Like us, they die with sorrow and in darkness. What advantage do they have over us? From now on we are equal. What will be within their grasp, and what will they see forever? For they too are dead, and they will never again see the light." I say to you, wrongdoers, "You have been satisfied to eat and drink, strip people naked, commit crime, acquire wealth, and see good days. Have you not seen the just, how their end is peaceful? For no oppression is found in them up until the day of their death. They perish, and are as if they were not, while their souls went down with sadness to Sheol.

## 103:1-15.

But now I swear to you, the just, by his great splendor and his magnificence, by his superb sovereignty and by his majesty, I swear to you, that I understand this mystery, that I have read the tablet of heaven, and have seen the writing of the sacred ones, and have discovered what is written and engraved on it about them. I have seen that all good, happiness, and honor has been prepared for you, and has been written down for the spirits of those who died justly. Much good will be given to you in return for your troubles, and your allotment of happiness will far exceed the allotment of the living.

The spirits of you who died justly will live and celebrate and be happy, and their memory will remain in the presence of the Mighty One from generation after generation. Do not be afraid of their abuse. Woe to you, wrongdoers, when you die committing wrong, and those who are like you say about you, "Blessed are these wrongdoers. They have lived out their whole time, and now they die with prosperity and wealth. They did not see distress and slaughter while they were alive, and they have died with honor, and judgment did not come upon them in their lifetime!"

When their souls will do down to Sheol they will be miserable and greatly tormented. In darkness, in chains, and in the flames, your spirits will come to the great judgment which will last for ever and ever. Woe to you, for you will find no peace! Do not say to the just and the good who are alive, "We were afflicted during the days of our trouble, and we have seen all kinds of trouble and have suffered many evil things. Our spirits have been exhausted, lessened, and diminished. We were destroyed, and there was no one to help us with words or actions. We were tormented and destroyed and did not expect to live day after day.

"We hoped to have been the head but we have become the tail. We worked hard and exerted ourselves, but we have been devoured by wrongdoers and the lawless, and their yoke has been heavy on us. Those who exercised authority over us hate us and goad us, and we bowed down to those who hate us, but they have shown no compassion to us. We wished to escape from them, so that we could flee and find rest, but we have found no place to flee or be safe from them. In our distress we complained to the rulers, and have cried out against those who were devouring us, but our cry has been disregarded, and they would not listen to our voice. Instead, they helped those who robbed and devoured us, those who decreased our numbers, and they concealed their oppression, and did not remove their yoke from us, but they devoured, weakened, and killed us. They concealed our slaughter, and did not remember that they have lifted up their hands against us."

### 104:1-13.

I swear to you, you just ones, that in heaven the angels record your good in the splendid presence of the Mighty One. Be hopeful, for formerly you were disgraced with evils and afflictions, but now you will shine like the heavenly luminaries. You will be seen, and the portals of heaven will be opened for you. Cry out for judgment, and it will appear for you, for an account of all your sufferings will be required from the rulers and from every one who helped those who robbed you.

Be hopeful, and do not abandon hope, for great happiness will be yours, like that of the angels in heaven. What do you have to do? You will not have to hide in the day of the great judgment and you will not be found to be wrongdoers. Eternal judgment will be far from you, for all the generations of the world. Do not be afraid, you just ones, when you see wrongdoers flourishing and prospering in what they do. Do not associate with them, but keep yourselves at a distance from their wrongdoing, for you will become associates of the hosts of heaven.

You wrongdoers say, "They won't find out about all our crimes and record them!" but all your crimes will be recorded daily. And I assure you that light and darkness, day and night, see all your crimes. Do not be irreverent, do not lie, do not alter truthful words, do not say that the words of the sacred mighty one are lies, do not praise your idols, for all your lies and all your irreverence do not lead to justice, but to great crime. Now will I point out this hidden truth: many wrongdoers will alter and misrepresent truthful words. They will say evil things, they will tell lies, make up great falsehoods, and write books in their own words. But when they write all my words correctly in their own languages, they will not change them or omit anything, but will write them all correctly, everything that I previously testified about them. Now will I point out another hidden truth: books which are a source of happiness, of reliability, and of great wisdom will be given to the just and the wise. Books will be given to them, and they will believe them and be happy about them. All the just ones who have learnt all truthful pathways from them will be rewarded.

## 105:1-2.

In those days, says the Lord, they will call to the inhabitants of the earth, and make them listen to their wisdom. Show it to them for you are their leaders, and the rewards will be over the whole earth, for my son and I will be united with them throughout their lives in the pathways of justice, forever. Peace will be yours! Be happy about the truth, you who have integrity!

## The Book of Noah - a fragment
## 106:1-19.

After a time, my son Methuselah chose a wife for his son Lamech and she became pregnant by him, and gave birth to a child. His body was as white as snow, and as red as a rose, and his hair was as white as wool, and long, and his eyes were beautiful. When he opened them, he illuminated the whole house like the sun, so that the whole house was extremely bright.

When he was taken from the midwife's hands, his father Lamech was afraid of him, and fled away to his own father Methuselah, and said, "I have fathered a son, who is not like other children. He isn't human, but looks like offspring of the angels of heaven! He has a different nature to ours, and is completely unlike us! His eyes are as bright as the sun's rays, his appearance is splendid, and he looks like he belongs to the angels and not to me! I'm afraid that something miraculous will happen on earth in his time. And now, my father, I beg and request you to go to our ancestor Enoch, and find out the truth from him, for he lives amongst the angels."

When Methuselah heard his son's words, he came to me at the extremities of the earth, for he had been informed that I was there. He called out, and I heard his voice. I went to him and said, "My son, I'm here, since you've come to me!"

He answered, "I've come about an important event! I've approached you about a disturbing sight! My father, listen to me, my son Lamech has fathered a child who doesn't resemble him, and whose nature isn't like a human's. His color is whiter than snow, he is redder than a rose, the hair of his head is whiter than white wool, his eyes are like the sun's rays, and when he opened his eyes he lit up the whole house! Also, when he was taken from the midwife's hands, his father Lamech was afraid and fled to me, because he didn't believe that the child was his, because he looked like the angels of heaven. And now I've come to you to find out the truth!"

Then I, Enoch, answered him, "The Lord will do a new thing on the earth. I have seen this in a vision and already explained it to you. In Jared my father's generation, some of those from heaven disregarded the Lord's word. They committed crimes, laid aside their race, and were promiscuous with women. They committed wrong, slept with them, and produced children with them. (52) There will be great destruction on the earth, a deluge, a great destruction for one year. This child who is born to your son will survive on the earth, and his three sons will be saved with him. When all humans on the earth die, he and his sons will be safe. His descendants will produce giants on the earth, not spiritual giants, but bodily giants. A great punishment will be inflicted on the earth, and all dishonesty will be washed from the earth. So then inform your son Lamech, that the child who is born is in fact his child, and he is to call him Noah, for he will be left to you. He and his children will be saved from the destruction that is coming on the earth because of wrongdoing and because of all the wickedness which will be committed on the earth in his days. Afterwards there will be greater wickedness than that which was committed on the earth before. For I know the sacred secret hidden truths, which the Lord himself showed and explained to me, and which I have read in the tablets of heaven."

### 107:1-3.

"In them I saw it written that generation after generation will disobey, until a just race arises, until wrongdoing and crime perish from off the earth, and all manner of good comes on it. And now, my son, go tell your son Lamech, that the child who is born is truly his child, and that this is no lie."

When Methuselah heard the words of his father Enoch, who had shown him every secret thing, he returned with understanding, and gave the child the name Noah, because he was to comfort the earth after all its destruction.

## Enoch's Concluding Words

### 108:1-15.

Another book which Enoch wrote for his son Methuselah, and for those who would come after him, and keep the law in the last days. You, who have watched and are waiting in those days, until the evil doers are consumed, and the power of the guilty is destroyed, wait until wrongdoing passed away, for their names will be blotted out of the sacred books, their offspring will be destroyed, and their spirits slain. They will cry and grieve in a chaotic wasteland, and they will burn in the bottomless fire. There I saw something like a cloud which I could not see through, as I was unable to look through it because of its depth. I saw also a flame of fire burning brightly, and things like sparkling mountains whirling around, and shaking from side to side.

Then I asked one of the sacred angels, who was with me, "What is this shining object? It is not the sky, but a flame of fire alone which blazes, and in it there are the sounds of shrieks, of anguish, and of great misery."

He said, "Into the place which you see, will be thrown the spirits of wrongdoers and blasphemers, of those who do evil, and who will alter everything which God has said through the mouths of the prophets about things that will happen. There will be writings and records about these things in heaven, so that the angels can read them and know what will happen both to wrongdoers and to the spirits of the unassuming, those whose bodies have suffered but have been rewarded by God, those who have been treated badly by wicked people, those who have loved God, those who have not loved gold or silver or other good things on the earth, but who gave their bodies over to torture, those who from the time of their birth have not coveted earthly riches, but have considered themselves to be a breath passing away. Such has been their behavior, and the Lord examined them and found their spirits to be pure, so that they might praise his name. I have recorded all their blessings in a book, and he has rewarded them, for they were found to love heaven more than their earthly life."

God said, "They were trampled underfoot by wicked people, and heard their abuse and blasphemies, and were treated shamefully, while they were blessing me. Now will I call the spirits of the good who are from the generation of light, and I will change those who were born in darkness, whose bodies were not rewarded as splendidly as they deserved.

"I will bring those who love my sacred name into the shining light and I will place each of them on their own splendid throne, and they will shine for unnumbered times." God's judgment is just. He gives faith to the faithful where justice lives. They will see those who were born in darkness thrown into darkness, while the just will be shining. Wrongdoers will cry out when they see them shining, but they go where the days and times have been prescribed for them.

# Chapter 3: Appendix A:
## List of Biblical References to Enoch. (53)

*Genesis 5:18* When Jared was 162 years old he fathered Enoch.

*Genesis 5:19* Jared lived for 800 years after he fathered Enoch and had other sons and daughters.

*Genesis 5:21* When Enoch was 65 years old, he fathered Methuselah.

*Genesis 5:22* Enoch walked with God after he fathered Methuselah for 300 years and had other sons and daughters.

*Genesis 5:23* Thus Enoch lived for 365 years.

*Genesis 5:24* Enoch walked with God, and then he was not there, for God took him.

*1 Chronicles 1:3* Enoch, Methuselah, Lamech,

*Luke 3:37* (...the son of Noah, the son of Lamech,) **37** the son of Methuselah, the son of Enoch, the son of Jared, the son of Mahalalel, the son of Kenan,

*Hebrews 11:5* By faith Enoch was transferred from one place to another so that he didn't experience death, and could not be found, because God had taken him away – since before he was transferred from one place to another he had the reputation that he had pleased God.

*Jude 1:14-15* Now Enoch, the seventh from Adam, prophesied to these people too. He said, "The Lord comes with tens of thousands of his devoted people, to carry out judgments on everyone, to cross-examine every soul among them who has committed sacrilege, about their sacrilegious acts, and about all the harsh things that sacrilegious sinners have said about him."

# Chapter 4. Endnotes.

1. See Appendix A for Biblical references to Enoch. The other two references in Genesis (4:17 and 4:18) are not mentioned in Appendix A as they refer to a different Enoch.

2. Jerome, *Letter* 181.4

3. For the pagan supernatural messenger (pagan "angel") context see inscriptions *ZPE* 30 (1978) 257 n. 7, and *EG* IV.210 (2nd c AD), as well as dedication to pagan *TAM* V, 1.185. The word also occurs in *TAM* V, 1.159 but it is not clear whether the messenger was a human or supernatural messenger. There is evidence for the term occurring in contexts where a derivation from Judaism has been ruled out. There is as yet no conclusive evidence as to whether the famous "Thera angels" were in fact Christian, cf. *IG* XII, 3 (1898) 455, 933-74, *IG* XII, *Suppl.* (1904) 1636, 1637 (Second–third c. AD).

4. Also known as "Grigori" after the Greek.

5. See lengthy discussion in J. Massingberd Ford, "'Son of Man – A Euphemism?" JBL 87 (1968), 257-67: Albright, W.F. and Mann, C.S. Matthew: A New Translation with Introduction and Commentary, (New York: Doubleday, 1982), pp. CLVI-CLVII, 95, G. Dalman, The Works of Jesus, Eng. trans. by D.M. Kay, (Edinburgh, 1902), V. Taylor, *The Gospel According to St. Mark: The Greek text with Introduction, Notes and Indexes*, London, Macmillan, 195, p. 197.

6. An Aramaic text reads "Watchers," Cf. J.T. Milik, *Aramaic Fragments of Qumran Cave 4*, Oxford, Clarendon Press, 1976, p. 167. Daniel 4:17 mentions a "Watcher." Nebuchadnezzar tells Daniel that he saw in a vision or dream a "sacred Watcher" who appeared to him and made an announcement. In the vision the Watcher concluded, "This announcement is by the decree of the Watchers, this command is by the word of the sacred ones, so that those who are alive may understand that the Supreme has authority over the human kingdoms, and he gives it to whomever he wishes. He sets up even the lowest ranked human beings over them." (From *The*

*Source Bible.*) The *Septuagint* (Greek Old Testament) translates the word for "Watcher" as "angel." However, Theodotion (c. 200 A.D.), the Jewish scholar who made a translation of the Hebrew Bible into Greek, transliterates the word. That is, he simply put it into Greek letters without attempting to translate it, as one does with names.

7. Other spellings of the name include Samyaza, Semiaza, Samjaza, Shemhazai, Shemyazaz, Semihazah.

8. Or, "On Ardis."

9. "Herem" was the practice of sanctification by total obliteration carried out against certain peoples, such as Jericho, by God's command, around the time of Joshua. See Joshua 6:17-19.

10. Equally possible from the text, "the assembly of El," or "the mighty assembly."

11. Elohim.

12. "Light bearer."

13. The Aramaic texts have an earlier catalog of the Watchers' names: Semihazah, Artqoph, Ramtel, Kokabel, Ramel, Danieal, Zeqiel, Baraqel, Asael, Hermoni, Matarel, Ananel, Stawel, Samsiel, Sahriel, Tummiel, Turiel, Yomiel, and Yhaddiel, cf. Milik, *opt .cit.*, p. 151.

14. Here the Greek texts differ from the Ethiopic. One Greek manuscript adds to this section, "And the women bore to the Watchers three races: first, the great giants who brought forth the Nephilim, and the Nephilim brought forth the Elioud. And they existed and their power and greatness increased."

15. Or, "and to eat their flesh one after another."

16. Often (mis)translated as "sons of God" (but the word sons/children with a noun indicates an association with the noun and should be translated thus), this occurs only elsewhere in Job 1:6, 2:1, 38:7, where it is clear these are angels.

17. Meaning unclear.

18. Originally Jewish, but preserved today only in Slavonic.

19. See also *Genesis 15:11*: "Birds of prey came down on the carcasses, and Abram drove them away."

20. *Apocalypse of Abraham* 13:4-9.

21. *Apocalypse of Abraham* 31:5.

22. *Apocalypse of Abraham* 23:7.

23. *Apocalypse of Abraham* 20:5.

24. J. Knappert, *Islamic Legends: Histories of the Heroes, Saints and Prophets of Islam* (Leiden: E.J. Brill, 1985), 31-3.

25. Qur'an, Surah 2:35

26. Qur'an, Surah 7:13-19. See also Surah 15:31-48, 17:61-65, 18:50, 20:116-123, 38:71-85

27. Abd al-Qadir al-Jilani, *Revelations of the unseen: Futuh al-Ghaib. A collection of seventy-eight discourses*, Abd al-Qadir al-Jilani, translated from the Arabic by Muhtar Holland, Houston, Texas, Al-Baz Publishing, 1992.

28. The place of honor (the south side). The Messenger was standing between the altar and the golden candlestick. At the left side (north side) of the altar was the table with the sacred bread.

29. Jude quotes from the pseudegraphical *The Assumption of Moses*.

30. The *Septuagint* says, "The one touched me with what looked like a human hand."

31. *The Book of Tobit* 3:8.

32. That is, Noah.

33. A rope, cord, lasso. Used by the Sagartians and Sarmatians to entangle and drag away their enemies, cf. Herodotus. 7.85, Pausanias 1.21.5.

34. *Porneia*, a term referring to acts condemned in the Law of Moses, acts encompassing idolatry and/or pornography, vice, certain sexual acts. There is no equivalent English term. Leviticus 18 lists idolatry and ritually unclean sexual acts against the laws of Moses, and in 18:3 states, "You must not do the deeds of the land of Canaan into which I am about to bring you." These included incest, sex with in-laws, sex with a woman as a rival to her sister, women or men having sex with animals, child offerings to Molech, sex with a woman during menstruation. Note also that the polytheistic Canaanites were particularly despised in the Old Testament, and male temple prostitution was part of their worship of their goddess Asherah. Cult prostitution and eunuchs castrating themselves (and thereafter dressing in women's clothing, cf. Deuteronomy 22:5) both figured in the worship of the Canaanite goddess Astarte.

35. That is, angels having sex with human women.

36. Near Damascus.

37. The plural of "cherub" is often written as "cherubim." Cherubs are described as winged beings. Numbers 7:89 states that Yahweh's voice spoke to Moses from between the two cherubs on top of the Ark of the Covenant. Ezekiel describes cherubs in Chapters 1 and 10.

38. Most manuscripts here read "not," but scholars such as Charles and Knibbs attribute the "not" to scribal error.

39. The Ethiopic word is *Ikisat* which means "serpents" and was translated by the Greeks as *drakon*, which means a huge serpent, a python, a dragon. The Hebrew word "Seraphim" can also mean "serpents."

40. In the Greek, *paradeisis*, commonly transliterated as "paradise," is a Persian loan word meaning a garden of fruit trees (or orchard) which first occurs in Greek in Xenophon's *Anabasis*, 1.2.7. It appears commonly in the papyri and inscriptions in the same meaning. See *I.Tyre* 1.108 (pl.47.1) (late Roman), "I solemnly request those who are going to acquire this orchard...", *P.Petr.* i.16.2.7 (230 B.C.), "the produce of my orchards", *P.Tebt* 1.5.53 (118 B.C.), "the tithes which they used to receive from the holdings and the orchards". *P.Lond* 933.12 (A.D. 211) notes a payment on account of an "olive orchard". See also the Rosetta Stone (*OGIS* 90.15, 196 B.C.). It occurs frequently in the *Septuagint* as a garden, sometimes as the abode of the blessed, see *Cant.* 5.13, *Eccl.* 2.5, and *Neh.* 2.8. The *Midrash Haggadah* (*Midrash* means a verse-by-verse interpretation of Scripture, and *Haggadah* is an interpretation and expansion of the non-legal portions of Scripture) describes Paradise in detail, as far as giving specific dimensions and furnishings of the chambers. The details are said to have been supplied by individuals who visited Paradise while alive. It states that 9 mortals visited heaven while alive, and that one of these is Enoch. Ezekiel's description of Paradise is similar to that of Enoch's: a great mountain in the middle of the earth which has streams of water flowing from under it. A palm tree grows in the middle of the center of the sacred enclosure. Similar descriptions are to be found in other apocalypses (e.g. *Apoc. Baruch*, 5, 2 *Esd.* 8.52). In Rabbinical literature the conception of paradise stands in contradistinction to hell. Paradise is

occasionally referred to as "the world to come". The word occurs 3 times in the New Testament: Luke 23:43, 2 Cor. 12:4 and Rev. 2:7.

41. Or, "When justice appears."

42. "The satans." (Same word.)

43. Job 41 describes Leviathan as huge, fierce, with scales on its back, states that it breathes fire and smoke, and that arrows and clubs have no effect on it, and that it stirs up the sea when it moves. Job 31 also states that there is no other creature like it on earth. Psalm 71:14 says, "You crushed the heads of Leviathan." The Ugaritic texts have the dragon with 7 heads defeated by the god Baal and by the goddess Anat. $KTU^2$ 1.3 3 38-39 and $KTU^2$ 1.5 I 1-3. Psalm 71:13 says, "You broke the heads of the dragon in the water." The dragon is called "Rahab" (proud one) in Isaiah 51:9 and Job 26:12. Isaiah 27:1 and Job 26:13 describe the dragon as "squirming." Job 41:19-21 states that the dragon breathed fire and smoke.

44. A vision of Noah and not of Enoch.

45. A vision of Noah and not of Enoch.

46. A vision of Noah and not of Enoch.

47. A vision of Noah and not of Enoch.

48. Scholars do not agree on the number of portions here.

49. Adam, the first human. Adam is a word which simply means "human." The above statement demonstrates the confusion between the English language and the original languages of Scripture. The verse actually reads, "God created *adam* (the word for the race of human beings) in God's image - God created it in the image of God, God created them male and female." Genesis 5:2 states, "God created them male and female and blessed them and called them human (*adam*) on the day they were created." The word "Adam" that we see in English translations of Genesis is merely a "transliteration", the result of putting the Hebrew letters into English letters. The translation is "human", person/s of both genders. Hebrew has grammatical gender. Many languages have grammatical gender but English does not. In English, we only use words like "he" and "she" when we are speaking of persons, and we try to find out the biological gender of those persons so we know whether to refer to a particular person as "he" or "she." In languages which have grammatical gender, all nouns, whether or not they refer to persons,

have a gender. Hebrew has two genders and Greek has three. These languages use pronouns like "he" and "she" with nouns, such as table, tree, and lake. The pronoun goes with the noun to which it refers. This is what is meant by "the pronoun agreeing with its antecedent."

We need to learn the grammatical gender of the noun to know which pronoun to use. It is exceptionally important to note that grammatical gender does not match biological gender - it may, but by coincidence only. Thus, in ancient Greek, the word for "old woman" is neuter gender. Yet if we were translating a Greek sentence about an old woman into English, we would not refer to the old woman as "it," we would refer to the old woman as "she". The Greek word for a trench is feminine gender, but in English it would be silly to refer to the trench as "she." We just don't do that in English. English is different from Hebrew and Greek. In Hebrew, the word *adam* is masculine grammatical gender. That means it has to have a masculine pronoun, just as the word for hand (even a man's hand) in Hebrew is feminine and must have a feminine pronoun. Again, this has nothing to do with biological gender. In the account of the *adam* in Genesis, Genesis 1:27 states, "God created human in God's image. In the image of God, God created *oto*." *Oto* is the singular masculine accusative pronoun agreeing with *adam*, the human. It has to be masculine grammatical gender to agree with the gender of the noun. It simply replaces the word *adam*. In English we say "him" because tradition holds that the biological gender of the *adam* was male and the English language does not refer to a person as "it." The verse continues, "Male and female God created *otam*." *Otam* is the plural gender-unmarked accusative pronoun. Grammatically, this refers to the *adam*, humanity. Thus the verse means, "God created humanity in God's image. God created it in God's image, God created them male and female." Thus God did not create the male first, God created the human first, humanity. God did not create a male first and identify humanity with that male's name. The previous verse, 26, states, "Let us make *adam* . . . and let them rule." *Adam* is here treated as a collective noun, agreeing with a plural verb, that is, the human race. Again, the account does not mention a singular male.

Genesis1:27 speaks of the creation of the *adam*. If the noun is a collective it could either agree with a plural or singular pronoun. That means that we do not know, from the grammar, whether the noun means "human" and thus the first human was androgynous (as the ancient tradition holds), or whether the noun means "humanity".

That is, we do not know whether a single androgynous "human" was created, or whether "humanity", males and females, were created.

Further on, the account consistently refers to males and females under the term *adam*. *Adam* is the general term for humans, both male and female. At the end of chapter 1, all the references to *adam* are in the plural. Genesis 2:5 states that there was no *adam* to cultivate the ground, that humans have not yet been created. The verse makes the point that humans are the only beings on earth that cultivate the soil. There is no reference to maleness in the verse. Genesis 2:7 tells us that God formed the *adam* from dust, breathed into its nostrils the breath of life, and that the *adam* was a living being. We do not know if the noun is collective or singular (as grammatically it could be either), and no gender is specified. Genesis 2:8 says God put the *adam* in the garden. Again, the masculine pronoun is used as it must agree with the grammatical gender, unlike English, where a masculine pronoun would indicate a male person. In verses 16-17, God speaks to the *adam*. At this point, the term *adam* still encompasses male and female.

In Genesis 2:18-19 God says, "It is not good for the *adam* to be alone, I will appoint a suitable helper for it." Again, the masculine personal pronoun in Hebrew simply agrees with the grammatical gender of the Hebrew noun *adam*. It is usually translated as "he" in English, as people have assumed that the *adam* was a male. There is nothing in the grammar to indicate that the *adam* was a male, and animals are first brought as suitable companions. There was no initial idea that a female of the species was lacking. There is no idea, grammatical or otherwise, that the *adam* is a male. In Genesis 2:20, the *adam* gave names to the animals. The *adam* here is now presented in the Hebrew as a singular person, but still there is nothing to suggest that the *adam* was not both male and female. In verse 21, God put a deep sleep on the *adam*, and withdrew the female portion from it. (Hebrew *tsal'ot*, Greek *pleura*, referring to the factor, the portion, it was only later Rabbinic tradition that had "rib".) In verse 22, God shaped that which he had taken from the *adam* into an *isha* (female) and brought her to the *adam*. In verses 23 and 24, the word *isha* (female) is distinguished from the *ish* (male). This is the first time the words for female and male have appeared in the account. The *adam* is now an *ish*, and becomes the individual Adam. However, the

123

meaning of the word *adam* has not changed, he is a human. Yes, he is now, at this point, also a male, but the word *adam* means "human." The female portion was taken out of the human, the *adam*, and became an *isha*. That which was left was still called a human, *adam*. Someone can remove a piece of pie from a whole pie, but the remaining pie is still called a pie. It does not have to be renamed just because a piece of it was removed. The following verse refers to the new two individuals as *ish* and *isha*, male and female. However, Adam as a name does not appear until Chapter 5. This has similar language to chapter 1, where the *adam* is created in God's image, male and female. However, this is followed by a significant statement. After the male and female are introduced, God blessed them, and named them *adam*: "God created them male and female and blessed them and called them human (*adam*) on the day they were created." Thus it is clear that the word *adam* bears no connotations of maleness. When the term is finally applied to the individual male Adam, it is the term *ish* which is used to note his maleness. Thus Adam is now a male, but the word "Adam" does not mean male, it still means "human". The Hebrew word *adam* did not refer to male humans in particular: it means "human," "humanity," and did eventually refer to the husband of Eve, but his name was "Human". Yes, at this point, he was a male human being, but his name was not "Male" in Hebrew, it was "Human."

50. A Qumran text reads, "Watchers and Sacred Ones," that is, Watchers who were not among the wicked ones, cf. J.T. Milik, *Books of Enoch*, Oxford, 1976, p. 264. Some differentiate "Watchers" and "holy ones" ("sacred ones") in Daniel 4:13 (and 4:17): "a watcher and a sacred one came down from heaven", but the translation there is likely "a sacred Watcher came down from heaven." (Literally, "a Watcher, sacred, came.")

51. The word translated "sons" with a place name, indicates inhabitants of that place and should not be translated as "son/child of..." The Benai Israel, translated in the KJV as "children/sons of Israel" actually means "members of the class of people called Israel" and should be translated "Israelites."

52. Here one Greek papyrus adds, "who are not like spiritual beings, but creatures of flesh," cf. Milik, *opt.cit.*, p. 210.

53. The other two references in Genesis (4:17 and 4:18) are to a different Enoch.

## Other Books by Dr. A. Nyland

#1 Best selling author and translator Dr. A. Nyland is also the translator of

### Complete Books of Enoch
### All Three: New Translation with Extensive Commentary (First Book of Enoch, Second Book of Enoch, Third Book of Enoch)

Many of the Book of Enoch books you will find are in fact public domain (the R. H. Charles version of 1917) which means that they can be given away to anyone for free, by anyone. This book is NOT one of those.

What is the problem with public domain versions? They are full of errors, as they are around 100 years old and have well and truly out-dated scholarship.

World renowned scholar Dr. A. Nyland has a doctorate in ancient languages and word meaning. She was a college professor at the University of New England, Australia, lecturing in ancient languages. She has appeared on television and radio numerous times speaking about ancient languages and ancient peoples.

These days, many non-translators sell the public domain version of 1917 by R.H. Charles (both as is, and disguised by slight rewording) as a commercial venture. This version reflects the knowledge of The Book of Enoch as it was back in 1917. Great advances have been made since then.

This (all 3 Books of Enoch) is a NEW (2010) and easy-to-read translation by ancient languages scholar Dr. A. Nyland and is NOT the 1917 R.H. Charles Public Domain translation of The Book of Enoch.

The Book of Enoch is of importance to theosophy and mysticism.

This book is an easy to read translation with cross references, copious background notes, and notes.

This new translation by Dr. A. Nyland contains all 3 Books of Enoch:

1) 1 Book of Enoch (Also called The Ethiopic Book of Enoch)

2) 2 Book of Enoch (Also called The Slavonic Book of Enoch, The Secrets of Enoch).

Also contains the extended version of 2 The Book of Enoch, The Exaltation of Melchizedek.

3) 3 Book of Enoch (Also called The Hebrew Book of Enoch)

The Books of Enoch are of interest to a wide audience: theosophy, mysticism. 1 Book of Enoch tells of the Watchers, a class of angel, who taught humans weapons, spell potions, root cuttings, astrology, astronomy, and alchemy. The Watchers also had sex with human women and produced the Nephilim. For this, they were imprisoned and cast into Tartarus. This is also mentioned in the New Testament.

In 2 Book of Enoch, two angels take Enoch through the 7 heavens. This volume contains the extended version of 2 Book of Enoch, The Exaltation of Melchizedek.

In 3 Book of Enoch, Enoch ascends to heaven and is transformed into the angel Metatron. This is about the Merkabah and is of interest to those who study mysticism and magic, and to Kabbalists.

People interested in theosophy, mysticism, or Old Testament studies will find this book invaluable, as will Rosicrucians.


## The Book of Jubilees

The Book of Jubilees is a new (2011), easy-to-read translation by Dr. A. Nyland and is NOT one of the many century-old public domain translations NOR is it a reworded public domain version. The Book of Jubilees is of great interest to students of antiquities and archaeology and is an important reference book for religious studies of the Old Testament and Apocrypha.

The Book of Jubilees contains information additional to Genesis and early Exodus, and is the account from creation to the early times of Moses. The Book of Jubilees claims to be told to Moses by angels when he was on Mount Sinai. One of the Dead Sea Scrolls, The Damascus Document, states that the Book of Jubilees reveals divine secrets "to which Israel has turned a blind eye." The Essenes, a Jewish sect who lived from the 2nd c. BCE to the 1st c. ACE, coveted the Book of Jubilees and kept it in their library. Jubilees are seven "year-weeks," a year-week being a period of seven years, so a jubilee is 49 years.

The Book of Jubilees is also known as The Little Genesis or The Apocalypse of Moses.

This is an easy-to-read translation of The Book of Jubilees translated into contemporary English yet at the same time has full scholarly references.

### The Gospel of Thomas: Translation with Commentary.

Written for the general reader, Dr. A. Nyland's new translation of The Gospel of Thomas contains both the Coptic and the Greek translations of the Gospel of Thomas. New Testament parallels are also included. As usual, Dr. Nyland avoids theological commentary, and the notes address solely the language.

The Nag Hammadi discovery of 1945 unearthed a complete version of The Gospel of Thomas in Coptic. This discovery made it possible to identify the Oxyrhynchus texts as fragments of a Greek edition of The Gospel of Thomas. While there is close correlation between the two versions, there are also notable differences.

The Gospel of Thomas is an important work for those interested in Gnosticism or Church History.

### Bestselling author and translator Dr. A. Nyland is also the author of:

### What were the Watchers?

This is an easy-to-read book suited to anyone with an interest in angels or demons. Ancient texts tell us that the Watchers were a class of angel who came to earth and taught weapons, spell potions, root cuttings, astrology, astronomy and alchemies to the humans living on earth. Some of the Watchers slept with human women. For this they were thrown into Tartarus and tortured.

Idioms such as the mistranslation "sons of God," which have rightly confused those who have no knowledge of ancient languages, are explained fully.

The book avoids theology, and instead looks at actual evidence. Find out what the Watchers really were!

## Nephilim and Giants.

The Nephilim, a word meaning Giants, were the progeny of the Watchers and human women. Greek mythology also speaks of Giants. The Nephilim were also connected with the Anakin and Rephaim. The latter were a mysterious group also known as Underworld dwellers. Most people do not know this, as the word Rephaim is translated in many English Bible versions as "the dead." Zecharia Sitchin, in a confusion of Hebrew and Aramaic, alleged that the Nephilim were "fallen ones" and confused them with their fathers, the Watchers.

Ancient languages scholar Dr. A. Nyland sifts through the evidence to tell us what we do and don't know about these mysterious ancient beings.

## Ancient Angels A – Z.

There is a huge amount of misinformation about angels on the net and in books. These provide secondary sources to modern books rather than to the ancient texts themselves. As a result, ancient writers have been misquoted over and over again and made to say things that they never said.

If you want to discover the truth about what the ancients actually said about angels, this book is for you!

## About Dr. A. Nyland.

Dr. A. Nyland spent her time on Faculty at the University of New England, Australia, teaching ancient grammar, conducting a lengthy replication of a Bronze Age horse training text, and drinking espresso.

She is the best selling translator of such books as *The Complete Books of Enoch* and author of *What Were the Watchers?* as well as *Nephilim and Giants.*

The information based on her books is not based on her own opinions, but is presented with a view to getting actual facts out there. This is harder and harder in this day and age with misinformation spreading like wildfire on the net, driven by all the books by authors who know no ancient languages, and get their information from English translations rather than the original texts. It is futile to research ancient texts in English translation.

## Be Informed of New Releases

If you would like to be informed of Dr. A. Nyland's New Releases or freebies, please go to **www.mysteriesoftheancients.com** and enter your email address on the form there. (Remember to click on the verification email which will arrive immediately – it might be in your spam folder.)

*Under the auspices of the Morrigu.*

Made in the USA
Lexington, KY
02 December 2015